More Critical Acclaim for
"SO SEE IF I CARE"

"By all means read David Crittendon's novella, ***Then See If I Care***.
It is a paean to the immortal Bessie Smith, known in her time as
"The Empress of the Blues." I believed the complicated woman whom
he made in these pages in prose that is as lyrical as her song. He has set
her in a credible, horribly racist early 20th century America, given her
a voice that at times conveyed the powerful brass of her sound, and at
other times was as tender as the most lovin' blues, and surrounded her
with three-dimensional characters who all ring true. I believed every
word."

> – A. B. Spellman

"A superb celebration of the Empress of the Blues! An inspiring read!"

> – Marilyn Chin

"As if the Empress herself were whispering in his ear, David Crittendon
writes this story of Bessie Smith as richly as she sang...and if I didn't
know better, I'd say that he was an eyewitness to her blues."

> – V. Kali
> *The Anansi Writers Workshop*

David Crittendon

THEN SEE IF I CARE

a story about Bessie Smith

David Crittendon
THEN SEE IF I CARE
a story about Bessie Smith

Dedication

For David & Susie Hawkins and Joshua and Ella Crittendon,
my grandparents.

For Doug Hales, husband and dearest friend.
Without his interest, support and championing my quest to write,
this book would not be possible.

ACKNOWLEDGEMENTS

My journey as a writer began in the early nineteen eighties, guided by the wisdom of the *Visual Fiction Workshop* of Patricia Cohan and inspired by the brilliance of my late friend, Samir Hachem. This book was born in these workshops, its growth nourished by Patricia's continued support over the years.

Bessie, the late Chris Albertson's seminal biography of the Empress, inspired me to imagine what Bessie Smith's life might have been like. What isn't fictional in my telling of Bessie Smith's life probably had its genesis in Albertson's remarkable text.

I also studied with Les Plesko at UCLA Extension. All who were fortunate to work with Les were saddened by his early passing yet grateful for his kindness and uncompromising devotion to the art and craft of writing.

My further development as a writer was nourished by: Dr. Lauri Scheyer of Cal State Los Angeles, *Statement Magazine*, Stuart Timmons, Mark Thompson, Rev. Malcolm Boyd, Peter J. Harris, V. Kali / The Anansi Writers Workshop, International Black Writers & Artists / Los Angeles, and C. Jerome Woods / Black LGBT Project,

Thanks to Dr. Rick Smith and Alisha Attela for guidance with pacing and editing.

I am so grateful for the good humor, generosity and publishing expertise of Andrew and Victoria Thomas of *Thomas & Friends Productions*, who shepherded me through the process of turning a manuscript into a book.

FOREWORD

Sometimes it is hard to name the exact event that changes a life, but Freedom Summer, seven months after the murder of President Kennedy, was this event for me. I volunteered to register black voters during the 1964 Mississippi Freedom Summer as a black twenty-year-old who had never been in the Deep South.

While I had struggled with Algebra 2 in a Midwest high school and dreamed of rocking on Bandstand with Dick Clark, southern black students dared to join sit-ins and freedom rides and demonstrate in support of school desegregation and equal opportunity in hiring practices. The determined self possession of those kids was unprecedented and their courage bewildered me. How could these students endure ketchup and spittle in their hair, and kicks and blows while singing songs of freedom and non-violence? Who WERE they?

These young shock troops of the Southern movement served notice that opportunities denied our parents and ancestors were in reach for our generation. They would not turn back or be turned around. Kennedy's vision of a New Frontier pledged change that was fresh and young.

At first it was comforting that the battle was far away, but this reprieve of un-earned safety quickly changed to self-recrimination. The music of resistance gleamed in faces that taunted the racist status quo and rendered it malignant compared to equality's exalted promise. I struggled to know their bravery but felt it was beyond me, unaware that courage is learned and earned through the example of others.

Meridian, Mississippi was hot, humid, treacherous. A few days before my arrival, James Chaney, Michael Schwerner and Andrew Goodman left Meridian to investigate a church burning in neighboring Philadelphia, Mississippi. They were considered martyrs by nightfall. Years of sheltering had spared me from towns like Meridian. I didn't tell my parents until I was already there. My Tennessee-born mother became hysterical. Looking back, her reaction was very rational: my life wasn't worth a dime.

The presence of mostly white volunteers sharing dangers usually suffered by Southern black folk caused the national and international press to notice "the trouble" in Mississippi. Many decades before '64, local activists had risked their lives to change the oppressive system. They, along side young activists and national civil rights organizations, had organized the Freedom Democratic Party to document how black Mississippians had been illegally denied the opportunity to vote in federal and state elections for nearly a century. Without this black infrastructure, summer soldiers like me could not have survived.

I recall eating breakfasts in the only restaurant believed "safe" for Movement people. It was a place where anger, tears, and gallows laughter were the norm, but where hearts could sail in the bright morning on a hub-bub of laughter and argument. On one such morning, the Impressions' *Keep On Pushin'* swelled from the jukebox. I put down my fork. The song was a favorite but this time I received its real message of resistance, community, and soul.

Next, a searing blues with a steady shuffle beat lifted me, gave me reason to believe I might yet belong. Civil Rights veterans, our mentors and heroes, sported denim overalls, "Freedom Now" hats, and gravitas. They karaoked Curtis Mayfield's sweet falsetto with determination and palpable grief. The recent disappearance was just one more outrage to be endured. The Movement, song and situation were one.

That moment was a turning point. Without this experience, *Then See If I Care* would not have been created. The experiences of those weeks caused me to leave the university, apprentice myself to the blues and begin the long quest for my true self.

Bessie Smith exists for most people as a touchstone, a name signifying a distant fame. Born in 1894 give or take a year in Chattanooga, Tennessee. She experienced an early life of black poverty with four other siblings, was orphaned by the time she was ten. Bessie came of age dancing and singing on downtown Chattanooga streets. She became known as the "Empress of the Blues," the first great star of the music that would capture the world.

I came to love the Empress as an adult after reading *Bessie,* the classic biography by Chris Albertson and listening to a reissued set of her Columbia recordings featuring remastered vocals that captured much of the power and nuance she had been famous for. Bessie's slow, commanding pace and transcendent, mournful voice settled in my heart in the place opened by the selections on the Meridian jukebox.

My book doesn't claim to be "biography." It is invention born of observation, study and love for a time period and its subjects. It's a long blues that places Bessie Smith in a starring role because for a time she held the key to the aspirations of a generation of black folk determined to live as free men and women. Though her heyday of 1923-1933 is past, Bessie reveals herself as archetype, unmoved by time. Within her performances are keys to the black experience, born in slavery, theft and greed, where new systems of spirit and sound had to be constructed if black souls were to survive.

Bessie lived the "life of a millionaire," achieving wealth when few black folk had material success. Yet she found fame insufficient for the breadth of her desire to be free and black. I understand her now as undeclared oracle, the destroyer of pretense and unearned privilege, but also as victim in the midst of renewal and lasting love. For this and so much more, Bessie Smith, the Empress, is the voice that will never stop singing.

– *David Crittendon*

❧ Chapter 1 ❧

I was born hungry but now I'm fat, every pound like money in the bank. There was always food but it didn't take much to make me feel deprived. Seemed like weeks passed since Mama made beans and dumped a newspaper full of broken pig feet, maws and snout into the pot with lots of pepper and sage. I prayed to get full off big bowls of soup without rice. I ate and ate and still was hungry but kept it to myself. It would have broken Mama's heart to see me dissatisfied after all she'd done.

Blue Goose Hollow on the edge of Chattanooga, Tennessee. Just cabins and gardens in the woods near Charles Street is where I come into this world April fifteenth 18 and 94. When Papa was living, the cabin seemed bigger than one crowded room, daylight showing through chinks. Kindling popped in a potbelly stove Mama prayed God to keep working. She prayed for more kindling to tame that bad wind rolling down Lookout Mountain, cold to the bone. Clarence, Viola, Tinnie, baby Bud and me huddled like puppies under three layers of clothes, old quilt stuffing wrapped around our feet, talking about "when will summer come?"

Folk say they want to know all about me, Bessie Smith, Empress of the Blues, because I made money and have that recognition they think is happiness. I tell them us Smiths were a flock of sparrows, not knowing apartness until we were forced to. No matter what Viola say, I remember Daddy. His voice and breath still on me, can't take none of him back from my heart. He did sing to me and hold me dear. We had comfort and loneliness wasn't worth a cent. We belonged to one another and that feeling never left me though so much is gone.

My daddy didn't have schooling cause of slavery always pressing down but he could read some. He did spade work and loaded packets at the river and we didn't want for nothing. Looked like we was moving up when the church got a big shed over by the bridge around 1900. Scrubbed it till there was no more bloody feathers and chicken stink. We were proud like it was a grand church on a corner. "Amens" and feet laid the beat from the back to front until the place rocked in solid time.

1

I never learned the name of that song they brought from slavery time. This was the beginning of it all, the reason you know my name.

I didn't know nothing but a brown-skin world. Imagine the shock when Mama first took me to see the white folk. They was smooth and pink and I wanted to touch their skin and rub against them like regular people. I brushed a white lady's hand and she jerked it back.

"The nerve of these downtown darkies."

"I'm sorry Miss, she knows better."

I didn't know what come over Mama. All the bowing and scraping. She never begged before. The woman turned sideways like she was looking back from the other side of the street. She whispered to the white man in the apron.

"Auntie train your child," the owner said.

Mama held me close and kept me from touching a jar full of striped sugar sticks. We stood by baskets of nuts and onions. I picked up a handful of pecans while she talked to the man selling cloth.

"I'm sorry, sir. She forgot her manners, sir." I knew I hadn't forgotten anything. I wondered why the nuts were sold when there were so many yards they could be had for free.

"Pay for what the girl got in her hand and you can go," the man said.

Mama shook the nuts from my hand then slapped me. It was twice the embarrassment to be punished in front of the white folk.

"Don't touch nothing you ain't buying," she said.

"Teach your gal before she come back, hear?" the owner said.

We left that store lickety-split. I never knew Mama to talk hard and fast as she did once we were outside. She burned up my legs with more slaps and nothing I said made her cool down. I hollered trying to understand what I did wrong.

"Why you touch that?" Mama said between swats.

"Because I wanted it."

"Stop wanting so much. Lord is my shepherd, I shall not want. Want the Lord. That's all you got to do."

Mama did ironing in a downtown laundry, was about six months pregnant carrying Bud, when a crate of pig iron broke on top of my daddy. You seen an animal chopped up after slaughter? People said that's how Daddy looked. We fell in a hole after that and had to dig our way out. I didn't pray any more like I once did. I knew the words but they just wouldn't come.

When Papa met the ground I called him with my heart, begged him to take me because there was no other voice I wanted to hear. Maybe I stood too close because death has stayed so near. After Daddy passed, I feared Mama might slip away too. I told her this but she said no matter what, we all have to stay our time. Just to ask broke my heart, but her arms held me like a song.

* * *

My belly puffed out like a new puppy's. I walked the Hollows determined to grub, hating the people who had chicken coops. Spring was on, morning glories, the sweet smells, clean sunlight, but I didn't care. If I had some coal I could trade for eggs. If I had some copper I could throw in some change for an old hen, but all I had was two sticks to beat ants with. I'd smell some neighbor's dinner and wonder how I could get invited in but nobody was rich enough for that.

My big sister Viola called the Hollows a throwed down mess only fit for niggers too poor to live in town. She wanted to move but Mama said no. She didn't want to see no more white folks when she got home. People say I'm rough but when you had a good daddy and lose him cruel, it's hard to stay nice. I stay ready to fight because danger's invisible as hunger and you got to meet it when it comes. All us kids prowled tracks to trails but no matter where we looked the future was what we already had. Might as well lived in a cave until it was time to work. At least the hole in the mountain would have been ours alone. Viola said my anger started when I got hit with a rock aimed at somebody else. Maybe so, but I believe it started long before before that.

Mama pulled like a teamster to keep us breathing but it wasn't enough. I couldn't stand having nothing but nasty grease to oil my legs, hoping my sister would outgrow a dress before it was too worn out for me to wear. Thoughts bumped each other while I hid a dime in the deep knot of a tree. That change seems pitiful compared to the money I've made but that knothole was my first bank. If a tree can grow leaves then I could grow pennies. There has to be an exchange between one hand and another to live good. Not everybody walk around half full wearing ugly shoes. New clothes say "look at me" but old ones hide by the roadside. I watched and wondered how it feel to know money is still coming day after next. Those white people in the bank always serious in the marble hallways. They see what they can do and then go do it. Their mind and mine not so different because one day I'm gonna have what they have. Big brother Clarence had already left town promising to come back with pockets full of gold.

I looked down at the river squeezing Chattanooga like a snake. Felt it squeezing me way up the hillside. Townspeople ate rich every day. I watched them choose their meat and cabbage, pointing at what they wanted, in and out of stores, my friends carrying their bags for a penny hoping a stray dime might mistakenly fly free. Dirty green river left the rich ones alone, but it came for my father when it was tired of muskrats and mice. I wanted a flood to claim the town though it could take our cabin too. High and mighty folks would have to watch the river like we did, hoping they could look at the remains they'd be given. These thoughts roosted like setting hens. I had to better myself, had to have some gold to build a home high water could never reach.

Mama thought I was evil at first, but finally decided I didn't ruin her washing on purpose. I tripped on sheets, tore holes in pockets, burned clothes with the iron because I just wasn't cut out for it. She let me run deliveries, go to school, and prayed I'd settle down. Long as I understood there never was enough money for anything, she gave me freedom.

4

Mama was thanking Jesus when I woke up. She should have been gone but kept holding Bud and made Tinnie swear to get Miz Watkins if her youngest got worse. The day was fresh with hungry birds, the sun huge in the trees. I unbraided my hair brushed it smooth to go with her. We shooed away chickens and goats and didn't let our dresses drag in the dirt. Mama's mind was tangled in the trees. She stayed close, her eyes everywhere but on me. Rustling branches and bird calls were the only sounds until she said Miss Sophie would fire her if she kept being late. I tried to comfort her but she pressed her hand against my lips, stroked my lifeline without a word. We greeted other scullions where the path changed to good streets with popcorn chains of lights still burning.

"Bess, promise you'll do right," she whispered through the cold air.

"Yes Ma'am, just the other day I dreamed the cabin held so much gold the floor broke. All us Smiths had pockets full of coin." Mama said prayer was the only dreaming she believed. Her feet beat the sidewalk like horseshoes, her voice low and dark.

"Think I'll always be here to warn you ?" She folded her hand over mine. "The rich man will chop your hand off before you'll take his money but Jesus listens with a golden ear. He calls me 'Darling'."

She was saying her time was nearly up. I quivered against her. I believe she heard my future tears falling, pressed her thumb into my palm to cool me, beat her fist against her leg saying "Yes, sir, yes sir," His will be done.

I gave her a look beyond my years and she caught it. Her eyes changed to grief but just when it seemed like she'd break, Mama shook off the blues with a snap of her head. She taught me that, how sadness change because it has to.

We watched the city come to life but Mama didn't care about horses dragging stones. She pointed to kids filing into the foundry and boys hauling water toward the road gang. I matched her stride that sped to a near trot. I didn't let her get too far ahead. She belonged to me.

Chattanooga was full of black men driving rigs, hauling every kind of load. We saw white boys running to risk an eye in the glassworks, a good job none of us could have.

After two streetcars passed, I realized Mama didn't have money to ride us. She didn't allow me to say anything; all the air was hers. She didn't allow boldness but I frowned to keep crackers from saying something to me. All of us stayed sad watching Mama stagger when blows caught her. When I prayed she thought I was talking to God, but I was begging her "Please don't go."

A double file of black men stood padlocked together beside a trench that ran the block. Office buildings already threw shadows in first light. The deputy unlocked the men beside a long wagon filled with tools. They were all ages and sizes. He talked hard and they took it.

Mama looked away but reminded me to do like I was told when we got to her job. Old men with spiky beards shook their legs like something might roll out. Young men strong as trees stood like soldiers. They leaned on spades and pick axes, wore metal collars on their ankles. They lifted the heavy tools, rubbed stiff hands together and stretched.

Mama said if she could doctor Bud a solid week he'd make it. Bud was dry, his skin clear as silk. No new cold spots on his lips after I'd held him the whole night. It was sad leaving Bud because he begged us to stay. We were half a block away when the lead man swung his ax. It had a beat that people don't remember now.

> *Ain't nothin' but a world of trouble,*
> *Trouble is all I see...*
> *Hurry hurry sundown*
> *Here nobody care for me.*

Men's voices echoed off the windows and walls, the leg irons clanked, lead man's voice high and strained like a squirrel running from a fire.

> *If I had listened to what my Mama said,*
> *Wouldn't be sleepin' in a rocky bed.*

If I could a-seen where the path done led,
I wouldn't have worms all in my bread.

Mama nervously opened the door. "I know who it is without looking. Keep it up and you'll be some begging coons."

Miss Sophie shamed Mama hard because we were late. She was colored but her heart was white. Mama stayed awake by working double speed, checked the glowing stove for the best iron to tame petticoats big as sails. I was doing deliveries when Mama heard Bud calling loud as a drum. His voice washed out the ceiling, swept tables away in a big wind. Miss Sophie said she'd hire a white woman before she'd take Mama back but Mama left anyway, flew past the hawkers and delivery boys, dared the wagons to run over her and only broke down when she saw Andrew and Tinnie racing to be the first one to tell her.

There wasn't any room but still the people came. Prayers and sympathy but no one tried to be cheerful. They put coins in a china cup and my big mouth was humble. Bud's coffin lay on the table for two days and nights. We pushed pallets together and tried to sleep while Mama guarded him. I hated the silent box. How could he change so fast? If the dead are with God, where do they meet? Mama said the pure in heart enter God's tent and read the answers in a book. She couldn't read but knew God would make it plain.

Mama covered Bud with a sheet when the visitors went home. We rested plates on our knees to eat. Tinnie wobbled her chair like wings but couldn't fly away. When I dropped my fork and knife, they sounded like bricks dropped on a tin roof. Just the coffin and some flowers in a glass. The petals glowed like a yellow moon.

"When he was alive, I left him to make that little money," Mama said. "Now he's passed, I stay home. Where's the sense of it? Why don't Jesus love me no more?"

"Have mercy Lord," Miz Watkins said.

Viola heard Bud's voice so we studied every rat-a-tat sound. She lit a candle but Mama couldn't bear the ragged shadows. I dreamed the

7

table that held Bud collapsed and I caught him like a rag doll. I rose from underwater, kept his head from hitting the floor. Lying on the table, he was finally my height. It was funny for a minute. He was clean nosed, soft lipped. I stroked his ears and forehead, studied every bend of his form as if forgetting one detail could erase his memory. I held his hand, promised my tears would come someday. Next day he was a bruise on the earth. We never had baby pictures. I've got a thousand publicity shots in a trunk but he's gone like a solo. A dream passing for a memory. So much has happened since he's been gone.

"What is it will save you?"

Mama asked because she wanted to fold me into prayer. I tried to tell her music was my prayer but she didn't understand. Still feel her hand on mine, see her flat-brim worn like she was born with it. Mama and I stayed close as sisters that last month, her words like rain on a leaf. I don't mention Bud much because time can't heal nothing. Losing his sweet sounds killed Mama. After she passed, there was no sense believing anything was going to the good. I churned like a top to keep from tipping over. Death put ice cubes between my legs. If I hadn't had singing, the pressure would have crushed me.

I visited the graves too often. Bud was buried next to the boulder with the green tinge, the rock that made me tremble. Mama and Papa lay just above him. After two years of rains I couldn't be sure where my people lay.

≪ Chapter 2 ≫

Viola gave up ironing for Miss Sophie to start her own laundry and tried to keep me off the streets. I hated how bleach stung but didn't argue. Any fool knows a nigger got to work but I hated having no time for music. Viola said Mama made her head of the family and we didn't argue when she lowered her voice to sound strong.

"Wake up. Sun's up and you sleep. Death creeps on fingertips silent as a snare, sweet as a dare." Viola sounded just like Mama.

"We orphans don't have nobody but ourself to depend on. Get your butt up." She shook us out of quilts, her anger on me because I was expected to pick up if she fell and falling was all she talked about. Vi never knew how much I cared. I was so afraid she'd die before I could make her dreams come true.

"What we got to eat?" the babies asked.

"Hot chicory and yesterday's bread. Shut up that crying. Bessie, lazy fat thing, suppose you gonna shake and holler on Thirteenth and Elm with Andrew. Think you white but Chattanooga will show what you is. I can't carry you all. I'll drop you before I get dragged down."

Her downhearted words tumbled out. I didn't blame her, only promised to pay back the years spent for us. Viola fussed and scolded to keep us from the pit in Dixie that swallowed black folk whole. We boiled and bleached, folded and pressed to live at the drop off's edge. Tinnie shamed me with sweetness, Lulu with her innocence, but I can't smile when life don't change. Hunger drove me to work the street even harder. I admired the show people most of all because they weren't stuck. Their destinations kept them free even if life was hard.

"Viola, it's not gonna be like this forever," I said, my face against hers.

"All you care about is singing and begging, Bessie. Nobody cares how much I got to carry. I'm gonna fool you. A man gonna take me away one of these days."

9

"You going to leave us for him?"

"I'm still a young woman," she said.

"What's his name?"

"Stop it Bessie."

"You going to have everything you want Viola. I'm going to put it there," I said.

"Anytime soon? When I die you'll feel a pain you don't know anything about."

Viola stacked the laundry until her face disappeared behind the pile. I tried to steady the load but clothes spilled on the floor. After Viola kicked me out, I raced into the yard between steaming wash pots toward town, my stomach against my spine, singing loud as I could.

Brother Andrew had it rough plunking notes on dead strings while crowds jostled and tripped him in front of the White Elephant Saloon. I pushed straight down on the moment, the beat in my right foot, stretched my back, shoulders loose, and crab-walked the chorus, singing at the same time. Raised my eyebrows 'til my eyes were sunflower size saying, "Give to the church. Poor little children ain't got a home." I danced myself dizzy, spinning fast in ruined shoes, trying to do better than yesterday. I worked Andrew hard but he hardly ever left except sometimes he'd wander off so sly I hardly missed him.

"Henry, give some money to the little nigger. I love that tune."

That's what they said in 1905 when they might give us a dime. We learned to look pitiful but still decent. If we were too dirty, might be taken for orphans and sent to a Waif's Home. Andrew's gimmick was to catch coins in the guitar hole. Every time the box moved, the coins rattled like bullets in a tub. No wonder I woke up scheming on music, money and fame.

The spot near the White Elephant had been ours for a good while so we stood our ground when two jugglers and an accordion player got there early and refused to give it back. The three of them was headed home

10

when Andrew, Short Leg, Pig Meat and I blasted them with stones and curses. Yeah, we were scared for minute when one of their boys played dead but don't judge if your grub's dependable. You'd learn to kick ass if it wasn't.

Andrew and I couldn't come home empty-handed because Chattanooga's East Ninth Street was full of hustles. Sometimes we ran errands to the back rooms where downtown men shot craps in the company of women free as swans who promenaded green and gold parasols that matched their stockings and petticoats.

We was poor but there was "broke-ass poor" like the Jenkins' who black-faced themselves to plunk a banjo downtown.

"We some real coons," they'd say. "Can't you white folks tell the difference between us and the pretend niggers?"

I didn't care what they did but it was pitiful how they never stopped grinning. One afternoon at the train station, Andrew and I played loud enough to give big mouths a headache. Why bite my tongue?

Won't you come home Bill Bailey? She moans the whole day long...

"Pay me now so you can tell your grand babies. My name's Bessie. Call the tune. If we don't know it today, we'll have it tomorrow."

A pretty woman stayed after the crowd moved on.

"Haven't seen you or Andrew in a long time Miss Smith."

She was about the first to call me "Miss" and I was real happy about it. I lied about why Andrew and I hadn't come back to school. Andrew whispered "school would be a jail in no time" and she heard it.

"You think playing low-down music is the way to succeed, young man?"

Andrew shut up. I looked away too.

"Bessie, please say you'll come back. This street is no place for a young girl"

11

She squeezed my hand with a sad smile. I wandered among the travelers wondering if the teacher was right. When the giant locomotives arrived, doors shook and ceilings quivered but nothing fell down. Steaming wheels taller than men turned then locked. Walls trembled like I did when the engines got pressure.

"Andrew, let's get on board and forget this town," I said.

"Why don't you go first?" he said.

"Memphis, New Orleans, Baltimore," porters squalled the names with mouth harp lungs. I walked double speed, free as a dream, hoping for a lost ticket, loving the gold letters on pure metal trains. I ran up the steps of a parlor car to stare at the luxury until the porter drove me out. In another minute I would have sat my black ass down.

I went back to school in time to hear about Yankees, Rebs and the Civil War. I pretended not to know about slavery but I'd seen the memories dance on Emancipation Day. If Daddy had lived longer, I bet he would have joined the brothers who rattled slave chains, wore Union blue and prayed for Lincoln's soul in a park.

Mama used to say, "We'd still be slaved without Father Abraham. That's why the Rebs killed him. Bless God you don't know nothing about a slave time."

I didn't keep up with my studies. Got full of myself because I could figure and write a letter. The teacher was right to say I couldn't come to school just to eat.

Chattanooga was thick with traveling shows and every one was better than a school lesson. I slithered under tents and crept many stairwells to learn from cakewalks and minstrels. It would take every trick to reach the top.

"Give to the church, my name's B-E-S-S-I-E. Nothing better on this street. Not today, not ever. Give to the church!"

"That's it, Sis. we're gonna have it rich someday."

I kissed Andrew so hard he ran away.

We wouldn't have made nothing that winter if Sam, the Shoeshine Man, hadn't befriended Andrew and let us hustle his customers at the train depot.

"If I was a young man, I'd climb this slippery pit before I drowned. Why is that teacher lady bothering you and Bessie about a school? What's a book gonna tell me about being a boot black?"

He looked to see if Andrew understood. "Girl's got more sense than a boy. It takes a crazy mind to leave and go."

"Why didn't you climb out?" I said. Sam's eyebrow wrinkled.

"You'll want more than you'll get. Life will trip you," he said.

SONGS

AS SUNG BY THE

BLACK PATTI

TROUBADOURS

M. SISSIERETTA JONES
(BLACK PATTI)

THE GREATEST
COLORED SHOW
ON EARTH.

VOELCKEL & NOLAN
PROPRIETORS & MANAGERS.

WORDS & MUSIC
PRICE 25 CENTS.

PUBLISHED BY
M. WITMARK & SONS.
NEW YORK — CHICAGO.

Chapter 3

Billboards were the first movies. I'd follow the man and his son to watch them slop glue on walls and big slabs of metal. They peeled white sheets of paper that exploded with pictures eight feet high, but nothing caught me like the playbill for "Black Patti Troubadours". Dancers almost twisted off the signs. Patti wore a towering hat with a buckle on the crown. Her picture made me believe gossip saying she could sing in Italian and French, and had a white French maid she couldn't bring to Tennessee.

Patti's foot dangled like a limb, her petticoats bubbling underneath, little foot pointed high. I visited like a church goer, touched it like a shrine. Yearned for yellow vests and smiles like cotton. I told my sister Black Patti was coming.

"She's so rich, people treat her like she ain't black," I said.

"It's just a picture you think is real and what about her money? Black folks here own houses they can't live in. There's rich colored in Chattanooga," Vi said.

"And we don't know none of them. Black Patti does what she wants. She don't stay and take it."

"Bessie, how do you know what she takes traveling all the time, no solid home."

"I'd love to go where she goes, see what she sees."

"Think so? She could be crying on a train, nobody to say a prayer. Better stay where your blood is."

"Is this house ours?"

"Daddy built it," Viola said.

"Do we have a paper saying it's ours?"

"Why you arguing, Bessie? You see a picture on a fence and next thing you're hell."

"Clarence said we don't have nothing, Viola."

"Clarence haven't sent a postcard or money in a year. Why you bring him up?"

"Ok, I'm going out to work Ninth Street," I said.

"Like begging with Andrew gonna make you rich."

"I've got to see Patti."

On summer weekends Andrew and I stood in the thick crowd around the "Doctor" shows that set up in a blind alley where white and black would gather before suppertime. The best hustler was a tall white man with coal black hair and striped pants. We watched him scare the shell games and thieves off his corner. Thought we were grown up, especially me, young beggars with holes in our drawers.

The Doctor worked a big-headed black man called Barabbas and an Indian Chief. Barabbas wore blackface with that white ring around his lips. He danced and played *Jimmie Crack Corn* on a tin flute, grinned and ran a bottle of remedy every time somebody said, "Here boy." The Doctor claimed Barabbas' own life was saved by the very stuff he sold. Fevers, gas, a broken heart was a thing of the past since Doctor found the secret cure of the Cherokees.

The Chief came on. His buckskin and feathers drifted like grass falling down. He stood tall, pointed where the sun was, and lit his long pipe. Drummed and sang his language while the crowd laughed but his eyes told the suckers to fuck themselves.

When the crowd was ready for the windup, Doctor brought out his daughter. She had honey brown hair laced with ribbons and a white dress we could nearly see through as she danced to music from the Doctor's squeezebox. Her ribbons and hair floated like milkweed and she never stopped smiling. Damn if the men didn't shovel more money to her in two minutes than we had made the whole day.

I said the white girl's cross steps weren't dancing. Just skipping and wishing.

"Why you care so much?" Andrew said.

"We're through until medicine girl's off the street. Please Jesus, put her on the dark road," I said.

"And you'll do what? Change her to black?"

The girl's whiteness set me off. I didn't care about her color but hated that it was all she had going for herself. Anger had me like a perch on a hook and wouldn't cool down. Some days I could sing past it but as I grew older, my anger did too.

"That girl hasn't done nothing to you."

"Why you taking her part? She ain't studying you."

Andrew walked off feeling hurt. I didn't want to face the street without a rhythm so I tempted him with plans.

"If we watch these white folks, maybe we can find a way to make more money."

The crowd cursed themselves for buying remedy, then took a deep swallow. Gambling began again. Ordinary folk prayed to shaved dice, fell for the chance to lose everything. Tired women saw how the daughter kissed her "father" and held their noses.

"I'm going to see if we can hook up with the Doctor."

Andrew reminded me that the white always cheat the black.

"Clarence wrote Viola saying we ought to go North," I said.

"That takes money," Andrew said.

"Don't you want shoes like the white boys? Smooth leather a thousand stitches at the sole."

He pointed to the bare feet in the crowd. I changed the subject because I wanted good shoes more than him.

"Wonder what Big Chief's really like."

"Ask him, Bessie."

17

"He's too smart for that. Got no reason to answer. Probably has scalps in his pocket. Planning to steal up on the white man, cut his throat and take all that hair. Scoop up that girl and marry her himself way out west."

"Maybe he'll take you with him," Andrew said.

There was a smartness in him sometimes, so I thought it over while I watched Barabbas work the crowd, tipping his derby, always grinning, repeating what the Doctor just said. He waved bottles constantly.

"Yassah, I was near dying," he said to a customer.

"Maybe it only work on niggers," the white man said.

"No sah, it work on everybody. The nigger, the white, Chinaman and Jew. It saved the Doctor's girl. I seed it myself."

"Gimme three bottles then."

"Yassah, thank you sah."

I thought of making remedy ourselves but figured we didn't have bottles or labels to make it look right. I pulled Barabbas' sleeve when he passed by. He ignored me but I kept with him until he noticed me. I was barely twelve but big enough to say "fourteen"; old enough to marry. I never noticed Barabbas' white gloves until we shook hands. He looked like a fool but his lips widened to a friendly grin. His neck and wrist were walnut complexion but his make up face had no glow, only a sweaty brightness.

"Mr. Barabbas, I want a job in the medicine show."

He snapped his fingers so loud I jumped back.

"I don't talk about my business, little girl."

"Me and my brother just trying to make it, Mister. Can't you help us?"

Barabbas leaned his face close enough to count the hairs in his nose.

"Knowledge ain't free."

"I don't have any money. I'm just trying to get some."

"Is that right? How much you need?"

"A lot."

"A lot? Hmm, I thought so. Run along, I ain't got time to fool."

"Please, Mister." I knew better than follow a strange man, but had to chance it.

"The Doctor and his flimsy daughter make good money," I said.

"Not so loud, girl. These folks listen when we disrespect."

"The Doctor need a helper?"

"The Doctor don't need nobody. Maybe I could find you something."

"When do I start?"

"Hold your horses, now. You haven't shown me how sharp you are."

"I saw the girl kiss the Doctor's mouth," I said, not sure if this was the proof he wanted.

"Ok. You watching sharp but let me hurt you: that child is no kin to the Doctor. She's his woman. Wants her so bad it's pitiful."

"How old is she?"

Andrew waved "Let's go" with his hands. He sawed his finger across his neck, then pointed toward home.

"Fifteen. She's grown. Think you could be like that girl?"

Andrew shook his head, "No". I didn't say anything.

"I bet you'd like a drink. A downtown girl gets thirsty."

I said it was play medicine and the doctor was a quack but inside I was thrilled because nobody had called me a "downtown girl" before. Barabbas took a closer look.

"Since you're too wise for the elixir, how 'bout home brew?"

He offered me a sip when the sidewalk cleared.

"No thanks," I said.

We were a block from the ballyhoo. Barabbas whistled two long two short. The Doctor waved his hat.

"Dinnertime. Some brew grabs your neck but this here is creamy like a downtown pie."

"Bessie don't want none," Andrew said.

Barabbas aimed a big finger at my brother.

"Atta boy," he said.

We slow paced into neighborhoods until houses thinned and weeds got thick. After he said I reminded him of a woman in New Orleans, his minstrel face felt more like a friend's.

"You're just the spitting image. Sure you don't want some brew? It don't bite one bit."

I fell for it like he knew I would. Andrew's warnings seemed out of place once that first high kicked in.

"Why should the white girl have a drink when you can't, Bessie? Ain't nothing but some home made."

He knew a place hidden by vines, a wild meadow studded by flat stones. I ignored the heat around my ears, my fast, shallow breath. Andrew followed us but I couldn't look in his eyes or listen. Barabbas suddenly lifted him like a owl on a mouse then told him to "get lost."

Barabbas stared at me without looking away. We were all alone.

"How old are you, Bessie?"

"Fourteen," I lied. My words disappeared between trees.

"You're small for fourteen."

"I'm no baby." Kept talking but wanted to hear other voices, even tried to leave but Barabbas herded me back to the big rock.

"I know you're a big girl," he said while he wiped paint off his face. "Now have a little more."

He put the cup to my mouth and nuzzled my throat so the stuff went all the way down. I gagged and coughed but still thought I had to do it. Heat waves opened and closed. His big arms worried me. He opened his shirt and showed me his chest. I didn't like his sweat on my fingers. I hoped it would rain. His hands on my arms and face.

"What you think now, Bessie?" Barabbas said.

It was a funny question because I was through with thinking. He poured liquor and I lapped it up. Sweet and mellow then fire all the way down. Clouds everywhere. I had no idea how long we'd been drinking. He peed on the bushes and turned so I could see it. I wanted to run but fell off the big rock, tried to stand but was on all fours, moved slow because the trees were changing places. Felt like I was flying out of my body.

"Barabbas, I got to go home."

"Bessie, have some more 'shine.' It's smooth like a lake. Like your skin. Ooh what you got."

I heard water breaking over stones. I took another drink, fell into the tub Mama bathed us in. My arms went rubbery. I talked to Mama like she was there. I let go my under clothes. My breast buds stuck up in the grass. He never stopped talking and touching. The ground was soft and warm, his simple talk a lovely tune. I hadn't said "no" since the world began moving. Somehow I was bathing with him. He unbuttoned his pants. Everything fell away between us. So much touching then his full weight on me like wood in a vise. His nails bit hard. A wedge between my legs tore and burned every time he moved. His lips over mine. My legs like logs. He wouldn't stop. Cinders, dust clods, stems stuck me. My neck knotted up, I breathed in little bubbles from the bottom, pinned to the ground with vomit in my nose. I got my mouth around his lip and bit clean through. Brought my legs together and kicked straight up. I tried to remember what standing was like. Air blew up my legs. Barabbas' shadow jerked up and down. His bloody lip hung free. Said he'd kill me then grabbed himself and moaned. I threw dust that came back in my own face.

"Get up, Bessie."

Andrew ran through the bushes and and tried not to peek.
He reached for my arm but Barabbas grabbed him. My brother fought
like a man but my head stayed full of rags, my arms nailed to the ground.
I had to move but my legs wouldn't jell. Barabbas raised off his knees to
stand then got tangled in his pants. I kicked sand until my legs gave out.
Andrew was smeared in blood and dirt. I grew more than stood, pulled
up by will, every step a champion. A dull broken noise and moans when
Andrew tore Barabbas' head with a rock. My left foot wouldn't straight-
en. All my weight pulled to one side. Andrew's footsteps sounded like
death. I said run light like a thief. Sweat cooled my legs and each step
made Barabbas' curses louder. Andrew dogged me to speed up. The trees
ran with us, the grass, the whole world was in a race.

"Bessie, he's coming!"

If Barabbas was close, I'd know. Could smell his ugly shit anywhere.
I'd brought Barabbas down like a slaughter chain but who'd believe me?
Hadn't been for Andrew, I could have killed the man.

"You didn't get Nothing! Nothing!" I hollered to Barabbas.

Andrew had filled his pockets full of stones. He wheeled and
chunked, birds scrabbling through brush. Yelled and tripped on vines.
Why didn't he shut up? I put Andrew in the dust. I'm no good
sometimes.

"Nobody can rule me," is what I said when they carried me in the
house. Sent sparks to the ceiling. Miz Watkins' voice spoke low and wild.
Always in my business.

"Is she alright?" Andrew hollered from the doorway.

Who asked him to be my daddy? I didn't need help. It didn't hurt.
I turned the tables. Barabbas ain't nothing. I was shamed by what
Andrew knew and saw. Only way to save respect was to act like nothing
happened and the more Andrew tried to help the angrier I became.

There was no music to hide in, only blood in my mouth.

My head dangled over the arms of others. If they stumbled I feared they wouldn't be able to pick me up. I wanted them to know I was beyond words.

"See what a hard head brings?" Miz Watkins said.

Flat walls, the sound of ripping clothes.

"Still think you grown?"

Her hands like trees, fingernails of wood, lye soap her only perfume. Naked again, she pried me open and washed.

"Cry later, Bessie. Cry when you give birth. See if you get wise then."

Crushed heat from the tub. Steam for memories, leaves and bark smeared in it. Covered and made to stand, the thousand wounds, funk of bedclothes, metal against wood, hushed voices. I feared Mama would return and her relentless voice sang all night. Daddy paced the roof. Bud's high giggle streamed through cracks in the wall.

"If Clarence been here, none of this would have happened. They lynched another man in Memphis. The papers said 'Negro Beast Burned'. Took him out the jail and the sheriff didn't do nothing. Might be Clarence on fire for all I know," Viola said.

I willed myself into future time where nothing blocked my path. Hard-head babies learn through trouble. Miz Watkins stayed between my legs, hard crust in my eyes, my body knitted by brittle cords. Bloody leaves came out. A footprint on my chest. One arm flopped like a wing. I had splinters in my tongue, sleep-walked while flat on my back. Tinnie's voice felt like music but words singed my lips and curses couldn't change the situation. My life felt over.

Andrew was through with me. If he knew where Clarence was for true, he'd have tramped to get there. I'll make it up to Andrew someday. Thought I knew what I was doing crawling down a hole with snakes.

"What if Barabbas comes back?" Viola said, and even I wished Clarence was home. Andrew sat on the porch with a pile of rocks, a strong bruise on his neck.

23

"Let Barabbas come, everybody die one day," I said

"Including you?" Miz Watkins said.

She stood up so fast, nappy braids fell out of her head wrap. Tinnie giggled and Miz Watkins gave a sweet smile of regret.

"Me and Jake had everything, but death came early."

Her eyes locked on mine.

"Things go wrong sometime, don't they Bessie? I got a pistol so holler if trouble comes. Reckon I'll make it in time."

She bustled out, knocking chairs with her big self, tears on her sleeve. The old lady couldn't turn against me even if I deserved it.

The neighborhood folks stayed away, their lives just sounds through the window. They knew better than to visit since half-of-them were happy I got messed up and the other half already been through it. In the morning I asked Tinnie for water.

"Why don't you get it yourself?" said Miz Watkins.

Didn't she never stay home? I walked to the bucket with short steps and gave myself a drink. The front door was slightly open. The world looked the same but I hadn't figured how to face it. Who would believe I fought Barabbas, left him moaning in the dirt. And, what did it matter? I was broke in, prime to be rode. Next day I woke wet with so much new blood I thought my womb had split. I cried then hated myself because I'd rather have blood than tears. Blood commands respect. Tears bring the sticky shallow prayers. I clenched my butt like Viola said and the flow eased down.

"Least you're safe from having Barabbas' baby," Viola said. "Just your period blood now."

I told her I'd kill it before it lived. Viola went pale.

"That baby yours too, Bessie!"

"Mine to hate. What kind of life is that? Too bad you couldn't have it for me, Vi."

"The child wouldn't have nothing to do with what happened. Can't you have pity for a helpless baby didn't ask to come into this?" she said.

"I didn't ask either," I said.

She slapped me hard.

"Don't you never talk bad about Mama and Papa."

She kicked me too, and I let her because that's what Mama would have done. After it was over, we both cried.

"Always trouble and disappointment and a broken-down house," Viola said.

A bright and fast movement flared outside.

"Look, I see Bud's face in the window," Viola said.

"He's been dead a long time," I said without looking.

"He's here, Bessie."

"No, he ain't. He's been here and gone," I said without pity. "He don't miss us."

Viola shook under the weight of what she knew. Andrew waved from outside the window. Tinnie held Viola's hand but I realized I was the strongest because I felt nothing at all. Why couldn't the rest of them face the truth? I had decided to force myself awake when a memory spoke. I bite my tongue when a tear falls.

A broken heart is like a Santa Claus. They're both false. I wasn't going to snatch glimpses of the dead out of imagination any more. The hole you're buried in swallows everything. They ignored me thinking they seen Bud. They wore his kisses around their eyes and felt a lot better for it. I had to be stronger than this to make it. A dick in your hole is real, a slap across the face is not a dream. This black skin don't change.

I peeled off the nasty covers. Every step a hell but I didn't shed the boiling tears. I shook so bad my shoulders ached. Viola put her fist against her mouth afraid I might stumble and break. This was torment I would come through like all the rest of it. I pointed to the big washtub.

Viola stomped to the porch and broke up kindling that barked like gunshots. Andrew fetched water without being asked.

I found Vi's whiskey and stood up straighter after it went down hot and raw. My head felt like a pillow. I couldn't stand the smallness of the room and the trouble I made. Mixed hot and cool water, spilled myself into it. Scrubbed and rubbed but memories laugh at suds. I needed more liquor and more food and more of everything the world had kept from me.

Would anybody cry for me now that I was broke in? I didn't cry when Mama died. Not even when the brothers and sisters walked with torches singing *Steal Away Home*. I didn't want to hear about a Great Reward long into the night. What reward did she find stepping off sidewalks, still grieving about sisters sold away? Daddy didn't say nothing about those days but we knew. I didn't cry next morning when the pallbearers laid her in rocky ground beside Papa and Bud. People say I fainted when the dirt dropped on her. I don't remember that but I hollered for Mama in that tub, lonely as I could be.

🌿 Chapter 4 🌿

Next morning I was through hiding. An early wind blew the door wide open and I was the only one willing to close it. Blue haze climbed the trees, soaked the bushes with light. Miz Watkins was still a busybody but I knocked on her door ready for church. I bathed in her surprise, put her arm in mine, tried to act right.

"Don't have to thank me. Fool 'em Bessie, try to live a long time," she said.

I felt full and strong with Miz Watkins, a big cork with pillow arms looked almost young but who could carry her if that bad knee gave out? She said Laurel walked with us on the long path edged by white-belle clover mixed with weeds. How many mornings had these trees covered us? A glimpse of the river's wild slopes and shrubs. The trail ended in a lot beside a big house.

"Fine things lead to greed. I'm so glad Salvation's free," Miz Watkins said.

"Or we wouldn't have money to pay for it," I said.

"I mean money can't get you in. Hundred percent faith. Ninety-nine and a half won't do."

She sermonized to signify with my mother because they both had come to the same idea: the world pressed down on black folk hot as an iron but the doorman to Glory left them a key. Out in the street, acquaintances better think before they call me names. I knew crib girls played out before they're twenty-five living like dogs chained to a post. They were the white man's lovers until he threw them back to the black. It will never happen to me.

Down through Cameron Hill the houses set back on grassy lakes. Miz Watkins worked for that one and the other one. Wide streets shaded by crooked trees. She could get me a respectable trade. I nodded and found holes in the brick walls, the nasty words carved on the fence. Miz Watkins recollected about the Civil War.

"I seen the colored swarm the city, the black soldiers and their guns. The sadness and the blood, the jubilation of thinking we was free."

She preached school and I promised to go back. The pain between my legs came and went. The good streets gave way to the big window stores and the rail line. I pointed at a Ford and said it would be mine before too long. Miz Watkins paid my way like she was my Mama. The trolley man said we could sit up front until the white people came but we stayed back, watched the city glide past. At Bushtown, a whole gang of colored got on and the wild laughing went all the way to the river. Miz Watkins waved and shook hands as the new riders came on. I threw hard looks before they could say anything. I spied some kids hiding in a doorway and could almost taste the liquor they'd found.

The Nickelodeon's white and red sign made me smile. Nickelodeon Girl, Queen of Dreamers. I wanted a movie of this street, every window and face. The light dust, the river, the shimmering coolness. Birdie, Mama's friend, got on board. I couldn't face her straight on. She hugged me, her heart timed to mine. She had one cloudy eye and said everything would be all right then tied a paper flower to a button on my dress.

"God's always near," she said.

I didn't say anything. The stores mocked us with things we couldn't afford.

"Your mama hardly spoke. Her hands were already folding and pressing like she could make up time in advance. I'll never forget that, how her hands were a blur and she was so 'shamed to be late'.

I wondered if I had the guts to start over in Chattanooga, Tennessee. Half the money in the breadbox was mine. Clarence's last postmark was Charleston and I dreamed of going there. We got off at Battery House where the trolleys turned back. Pure cream clouds above the bridge. Low bluffs to the water, wide steps down to a beach of beaten dirt. The boardwalk thick with couples running after kites, boys selling candy and pigeons. Back then, vendors sang their hustles instead of printing up a sign. If you couldn't sing, you wouldn't sell. Boats headed for picnics on Shell Mound. People swarmed us, always "hello" never "goodbye". White robed deacons washed feet while the members clapped. Preachers baptized sinners for a long count in the cold water. My mind changed direction. I wanted to be washed clean but none of the clothes I wore were mine.

Miz Watkins worked her way up front. I dawdled because I didn't want to talk to women wearing hats big as shade trees. A boy I knew spied me and got too familiar.

"Bessie! Heard you got broke up bad. People say Barabbas took..." I nearly skinned him alive, smoothed my skirt and forgot he ever lived. Prayers fell against the sand. Mama was there somehow. I was ashamed about doubting Bud had been at the window. I searched for him like a prize in the sand. The preachers led the sinners into waist high water. When they hit the river their robes clung like spirits. Miz Watkins saved me so I sang the gratitude I couldn't put in words. I heard my true voice, my own tone bounced back by the wind. It sounded so good I didn't recognize it was mine at first. I stepped into a chant and swayed like a floating bridge. A stout nervous woman sang to the baptized and I followed her. She paced the beach, one finger toward heaven and the drifting birds. Summer lightning burst over the river. Before that day, simple hunger owned me, but now I was satisfied. Never heard my own yearning until this woman singing *Steal Away* planted herself before me. I echoed everything she phrased. My song billowed out to the boardwalk, then returned. Sounds I'd only imagined now caused the rich to walk from the white beach to our side. I dared the voice to disappear but it went wherever I sent it. I plowed the beach with a sound thick enough to stand on. It weighed something. Heavy, then light, older than I was. A trumpet with lots of bass. Think they didn't wonder how a girl doomed to be a coke head monkey woman chained to a hell hound's dick could have such power?

I willed more people to come. The biggest crowd I'd had and no Andrew to pass the hat! I knew this sound was going to be gold. Even tasted the cool soft metal but my big sound suddenly turned small and caught. The church sisters talked me through. They wouldn't let me fall now that they'd seen me rise. If I failed to find the song again, their laughter would scald me. Right then a bolt of sound poured from me like rays from a lamp. Long as I sang from the edge of tears there was no need to doubt my voice. I could start fresh, forget being naked in the dirt. It couldn't last. I lost the woman who sang to me. Searched from the river's edge to near the landing where Second Hand and Orphan Girl schemed with a pickpocket.

"Leave the church folks alone," I warned.

My pals said I looked pitiful in my sisters' hand me downs and next time to grease my knees before I suck dick. I put my foot so far in their ass Jesus couldn't pull it out. Orphan Girl's throat was mine when the Peanut Man pulled me off. He had a tooth crowned in gold and sang his words more than spoke. The Peanut Man charmed me like a snake, led me still cussing past the crowd.

"That's a girl, let it all out."

* * *

I knew I was being watched.

"Pretty good for a girl," Andrew said from behind me. I hugged him, remembered how he saved me, laid my head on his collar, saw the ragged tear at his hairline.

"Every time I run, it hurts," Andrew said. His face was close enough to kiss but I hung my head instead because he was still solid with love I didn't deserve. I left knowing joy and tears were a single taste in my mouth. So what if the whole town saw me torn and drunk? I know a loneliness they'll never find. If one of them put something in me when I couldn't remember; better never let me know.

"Where you think you're going?" Viola said later that evening.

"You know, Ninth Street, make some dimes," I said.

"Didn't something happen to you because of Ninth Street?"

"That man didn't get nothing. I didn't have no baby. He didn't get nothing."

"You're crazy."

"Barabbas got me nervous but I ain't scared."

"I'll pray for you."

"Nobody safe until Judgement Day, Vi. Mama said we live on a raft in a churning sea. So be it. Then see if I care."

32

❧ Chapter 5 ❧

One afternoon at the train station, Andrew and I and sang loud enough to give loudmouths a headache. I was thirteen and not studying the past. I wasn't a grownup but it was near about time.

All I needed to draw a crowd was open my trap.

Ragtime was the rage, the bread and butter of show biz. Sometimes the songsters would catch our act on the street. They knew my intentions before I did.

"Don't even ask to run away with us, Bessie. You're too young."

"Too young for what?"

"If you got to ask, you ain't coming."

"I'm older than I look."

Laughter, a tip, everything was "next time," or "keep like you're doing." Guess they thought I was going to live forever.

Barabbas didn't return. Dark streets worry me even today but fact is Barabbas didn't get much and I hurt him bad. Clarence almost got him in Georgia. Mr. Outlaw got soft around me after what happened. He swore Barabbas was dead if their paths crossed, then put a whole dollar in my hand.

"I been watchin' you all these years."

"You sound like the police."

"C'mon, girl, police is the last thing I am. Other kids hit a lick but you mean business. You sing more than you have seen."

"I've lived plenty, Mr. Outlaw."

"Don't mean no harm, Bessie. Take your time, leave some room for the days ahead."

* * *

The soft weather soothed me, lulled me into a sleepy kind of living that can't be trusted. It was the pure end of autumn, gullies and ridges heaped with leaves and vines. I was the first to smell trouble but it was Tinnie who left the yard and saw smoke. Miz Watkins thought it was nothing but a bonfire, but made us go see. We found a cabin burning and heard children wailing but couldn't do nothing but send Andrew to the firehouse. A hot mist rose and fell. Little fires exploded. Hot cinders gathered like they had a plan. I tried to tamp them out in smoke thick as bees. The wailing stopped. I feared the strange smell might be burnt children. Afraid the earth might fold and take me down. There was no time to save anything but ourself. We hobbled down the hill knowing everything in Jesus' hand. Andrew begged the firemen but not one of those pumpers risked a horse for us.

Instead, they soaked big trees in Cameron Hill with so much water kids sailed boats in the gutter. A lot of townspeople came up to gawk and "tsk tsk." Viola, on her way home, saw the chief writing his report like he had done something. The ground was stove hot the day after. Our hopes collapsed, a vision of what my life might hold worried me.

"Look around," a voice told me. It wasn't the sound of God that Daddy preached about. A cold even tone, pure wind forced into a bell.

"Look and see what?" I wondered. A slice of moon slipped through the haze but night had us. Blue Goose Hollow had burnt up. People wild about money roasted in a coffee can. The roof of our place fell in. The back wall, a lean-to. Nothing left but the stove, dishes, a trunk of clothes. Viola couldn't be touched.

She said "What are we supposed to do?" over and over. Walked into the smoking yard. Kicked the burnt mattress. She knocked over anything that stood and laughed when it fell. Miz Watkins said we'd learn who our friends was now. Men swore they'd rebuild, but dreams die. I puked in bushes covered with ashes.

"Nothing will stop me," I said again and again.

"We can't even make a pallet on the floor. We don't have a floor. We don't have..." Viola said from her broken heart.

34

"Living is just another name for disappointment."

"Money will make the tears taste sweeter," I said.

Miz Watkins said I shouldn't make a religion out of money.

"Why are you afraid money will ruin us when you see what poverty has done?" I answered.

"If you get it, the white will take it back. They don't want us to have nothing," Viola said.

"What if I don't let them take it?" I said. "What hope would die tomorrow? Would we split up like slavery time and not see each other again? I'd hobo like a man before I'd live by the side of the road in a box made for turnips."

I swear the fire spoke.

"All this is past. Get inside before the snow falls. After while, you won't even try to find where your people are buried. The marked trees are gone."

Tinnie and Lulu cried "hungry" while Andrew sifted through what we used to call ours. I stared at ruined trees. When the two children were found in the ashes, sobs crushed the curses around the bonfire. The kids' stepmother hollered like she'd stepped on a nail. She even fainted, but the boys' daddy let her fall because she didn't love his first woman's babies no way. It was pitiful to hear her beg to be picked up from the ground.

Years later, riding in my Packard, waving at people who thought they'd seen a maid joyriding, the night of the fire will come back to me. In spite of the success and fame, those years in Blue Goose Hollow were the best of all. Daddy and Mama held me like a bird in a nest. Rising early Sunday like any day, water boiled for mush, got us up and out, our shabby best pressed like it was silk, then paraded us like geese all the way to church. It wasn't easy but then what is?

Everything changed when the family moved downtown. Looking back, it was all the difference. After that, days were pulled behind a fast train. I look back and understand it now that everybody knows my name.

35

The reason I spoiled Viola and Tinnie was because, after all, they cried for me. They were going to have plenty of everything because I saw future time real as our cabin with rags stuffed in holes and paper windows. I told them white and black would pay to see my hips move. After it came to pass, my attitude was "Why did it take so motherfucking long?"

Viola couldn't wait to leave the Hollows. For once, I just wanted Viola to tell us what to do. A wagon filled with what was left rolled toward the good streets. A pig was tied to the tailgate, two squawking hens lashed to the side. I thought eating chickens was a good idea but the owner didn't. Nobody's clothes fit. We wore what was dry. Red-eyed, scratched and cut, our world was a fireplace.

My family and Miz Watkins had decided to throw our rags together and "make a quilt" downtown. A lot of clothes flew off but nobody cared. I was young enough to believe losing everything would make me stronger, amazed we moved so slow and yet stayed so uncomfortable. The wagon nearly tipped when we left the dirt street onto Cameron Hill, paved and cool. Our slowpoke wheels angered fast drays hauling goods. Gutter-sifting white boys jeered but nobody threw rocks. The stink of fire draped our side of town. We rolled to Gateway Avenue, crossed the tracks where old houses crowded the sidewalk, and life stayed busy as could be.

❧ Chapter 6 ❧

Miz Watkins called out to a two-story house next to a fence plastered with bright colored Black Patti posters that became my reason for living. Her friend let us use the attic and even gave Miz Watkins a bed downstairs. I sat in the strange house and remembered the soft dust of the wildwood. The shoe box attic had a window that was too dirty to see through, but we all tried. It was hell bumping heads, knocking over piss jars in the dark, making do in a stranger's home. Viola said we were lower down than ever but she was still Queen Bee. She and Miz Watkins went back to washing clothes while Andrew and I stayed in the street. He walked pails of beer and packs of gage from one joint to another while I played nursemaid in the whores' bedrooms. I saw everything too young but how could it been different? The smell of sex and fifty-cent tips kept us living decent.

* * *

Later that month, I spied "Black Patti's Troubadours" on a rail car. By noon, Patti drew a crowd big enough to stop downtown traffic. Colored musicians in maroon suits, gold stripes down the legs, sharp military caps, eyes straight ahead. Trombones, trumpets, snare drums whistled with light.

Five carriages with matched horses pranced and paced. A surrey with a leather bench came last. Bass drum thumped, snares trembled. The colored conductor cued march time. A gang of light skin women in peach gowns and parasols cakewalked with men in suits. They were the sharpest browns I'd ever seen. A blacked up Rastus Brown waddled out wearing ridiculous shoes, pretending to eat a cardboard slice of watermelon. Behind him, seven foot tall King Solomon, followed by Slim, Tom Thumb in waistcoats and soot. The little one juggled, Solomon dipped and bent his body like bamboo in a storm. A new roadster wheeled across the the trolley tracks.

"You mean a nigger's gonna ride in that?"

The railcar door opened, a red carpet on the steps. Patti stood and waved, dark as her name. A valet helped her step to the street. Her hair rose and fell, a silver necklace, an airy gown sported medals and ribbons. I feared she'd trip but she moved like born-to-money to her car, still waving like the mayor. The city was dumbfounded. Negroes so slick white people looked poor, so you know what seeing this did for me. The parade ended at the Opera House. The orchestra conductor played the song on his fiddle Patti would sing that evening because "Madame Patti does not sing on the street."

"Who she think she is?" was said, but plenty paid to find out. I learned years later she hated being called "Black Patti" because her real name was Sisseretta Jones, and nobody knew her by that. I slipped into the Opera House rehearsal to hear notes like fireworks, tones fat as ripe fruit. Her music was too rich for me but her voice made my ear drums hum. If I had that sound, even half of it, I'd be number one. Tinnie would have time for school, Lulu, Andrew, all of us would wear good clothes and have plenty of food. Clarence would take care of the money. I would pay back Viola like I promised. There would be enough to not worry about tomorrow. I could hear the preacher say "Peace, be still and know I am God" and not doubt one word.

❦ Chapter 7 ❧

We sat high in the Buzzard's Nest for Patti's big show and the white ground floor seats was open to us for one night. Downtown men took the box seats until the ushers forced them out. No colored had been allowed in the Opera House before, and weren't welcome again until I got famous ten years later. I knew Patti had New York money because the backdrops and props looked real from just ten feet back. No painting on sheets and homemade costumes for her. This show pranced and clicked its feet. The actors who played the henpecked husband, the bitch wife, smart aleck son, and a mean mother-in-law had show business figured and sold.

Actors stuffed into animal costumes made children squeal and climb the back of seats. Live monkeys on leashes caused clouds of peanuts and candies to tag the stage and orchestra. I heard a fiddle player say, "the same country niggers everywhere you go." Monkeys skidded on their itchy butts while the crowd laughed and pointed but the animal's frightened eyes sent me low.

Some folks felt the second half couldn't top the first but I stood when the music began like the flag was being raised. The orchestra played "longhair" too long, but we held our breath when the hall went black except for a burning spot. The curtains parted. Patti had golden threads in her hair! Diamonds spit rays off her crown, a velvet robe clung to her shoulders, swirled to the floor like a statue. She got applause just for standing there. The voice from the rehearsal blasted the theater with heat and pressure. I worried as Patti climbed the scales, afraid she'd miss the high notes, the very tones that made the crowd stomp their feet and cry. She and the other singers romanced, argued and fought until the tenor was stabbed by his rival after singing mad love to Patti. She cradled the dead man's head in her lap and sang the sweetest and angriest tune I'd ever heard. The colored were beside themselves when it was over. We wouldn't stop whistling, pounding the floor, the backs of chairs. Patti made us wait for the encore, returned with just the piano player to sing *Feel Like A Motherless Child*. I thought please don't sing that song.

She ended on a held note, a sound whistle-high that dropped to a whisper, held that softness so long I couldn't keep from crying.

Some thought Patti was *dicty* because she sang opera. They could kiss my ass. If she wasn't rich and free from tears as she looked, at least I wasn't wrong about her beauty. She was black, dressed like a princess, riding in a fancy car. I rushed backstage and stumbled my words but Patti squeezed my hand like she already knew what I was trying to say.

* * *

Just when things settled down at the new place, we were accused of bringing lice and had to move. We scrubbed the whole house just to keep peace but by week's end we were fortunate to afford a dingy flat in a three-outhouse building. Rows of houses and no trees. Streets that became glue in the rain. Our porch was a basin throw from the next house. We hung clothes indoors to keep smoke and dust from ruining our washing business. I scrubbed sheets reliving how Patti stepped from the train, jewels in her ears, wearing clothes only queens could afford.

I annoyed Viola and Tinnie by pretending we could have different outfits each day of the week.

"Are you out your mind?"

"We need suits and necklaces, real pearls in a velvet box. I went in that store people your color ain't allowed and tried on three dresses."

"Wonder they didn't arrest you for stupidity."

"That's true. But if I was Patti, they'd act altogether different."

I spent a lot of time pretending to be rich, sure that when I got to be somebody, sadness would disappear down my gold-plated drain. Ten hour wash days left only Saturday afternoon to street sing and hustle. I could memorize songs after a couple of hearings and mock the local singers to a T. The Star Theater let me sell popcorn. To get onstage for a minute, I became a prat falling, pillow-stuffed fool, bawling mock tears with a happy heart. And, of course there were errands.

"Listen here, Bessie, run this package over behind the saloon. Just ask for 'Little Bit.'"

Someone peeked around the door soon as I hit the front step.

"You got somethin' for me?"

The woman was naked under her slip, A man snored in the bed. I gave her a small, dark brown bottle. I saw but didn't see, heard but didn't tell.

"Sit over there," she said. "I know he got some money."

She went through the john's pants, gave me a dollar, stuffed some bills under a lamp.

"If you want real money you got to give up that singing. You got a lot to work with already. When you're sixteen, busting out where the men like it, you could own a building in five years' time," she said.

I got drunk with one girl and watched her change clothes. I let her rub me with perfume. I was tempted to join a stable but saw that whores were slaves no matter what they thought.

My brother Clarence finally came back in town, misunderstood what I was trying to do and ruined my name with the easy riders.

"You want to sing or just hustle your way?" he said.

"I don't turn tricks. I just deliver," I said.

"Keep up with the dancing. There's other ways to make it besides carrying coke and tempting fate. Look at me, girl."

"I'm looking, Clarence."

"Show business jobs are opening up. You can get in it. Everybody knows you have talent. Half the Negroes in Chattanooga have given you a coin more than once. I'll send for you once there's a chance at something. Don't make me bust a crib and shoot a nigger. You understand me?"

We were nose to nose. He scowled like he was going to strike but that was not his way. Viola got pregnant, but God knows when because she even worked in her sleep. We washed and cursed while Viola swelled into a melon. Thought she'd have twins at least and strictly kept myself out of the boy-girl business. Viola warned "time marching on," called me "funny" for saying a baby wasn't "everything" when her life was nothing but laundry soap and other people's clothes. She and Miz Watkins had the cleanest hands in town. The old lady needed to rest more and more, but all that ended when the baby came and she had to bear the full load of keeping the laundry running.

Playing and singing went to hell while I bleached, folded and listened to the old girl preach and teach Viola how to be a mother. We held on until Miz Watkins got the letter inviting her to live in Mississippi and Viola's pleas couldn't change her mind. We watched Miz Watkins iron faster than any two people. Old and broke down, there was no replacing her.

"You gonna make it, Viola. You feel you can't do it without me but you lost your Mama and made it through."

"I made it because of you," Viola said.

"Everybody got to stand on their own and you can too. I'll pray for you all but it's time for me to go."

She gave Viola a knotted handkerchief full of coins on that last day.

"It ain't much but it's got a lot of love in it," she said.

All us Smiths and a bunch of the church folk were there when she stepped on board. We knew this was the last time. My heart sank when the engine stoked up steam. Andrew got inspired to pat Juba rhythm on his knees and chest. I danced around hollering "Give to the church" between verses like I always did. Viola was embarrassed by the church people's frowns but Miz Watkins called to me as the wheels slowly turned. If anybody took Mama's place in my heart, it was Miz Watkins, but I didn't see it until that day. I ran streaming tears, words lost in the train's roar.

"You keep on, bad little black girl," she said, leaning out of the window, her hand on her hat as the train rolled south toward the wooded valley.

"You keep on."

Chapter 8

Cora Fisher liked liquor straight and didn't smile every time a man did. The horn player leaned forward, pleading an alibi. A mood so black and blue I thought stems and roots might spring. The guitarist kept straight chunk-chunk time that Cora swung against. The falling notes streamed among us. The cornet melody said "laughter brings tears."

Been so lonesome, I could cry
Been so lonesome, been so lonesome
Eyes too tired to cry
If you don't come back, Daddy,
Don't care if I die.

Then she sang

I hate to see that sun go down
Knowin' you'll never come 'round

When she stopped, damn if I didn't feel heat. Cora sang mid-tempo, confessed heartbreak to a room full of people and it seemed alright. I forgot it was a performance. A blue remorse got loose. She made me shimmy like an African. Pure voice streamed from feet to her mouth. I was a pest after that. Ran errands for free to learn that magic. She didn't trust me but figured what I wanted couldn't be stolen.

"The blues found me at a funeral. I learned that men sing to keep from crying but women sing, cause we can't help it," she said.

Cora knew it was a compliment when she heard me say "I see pictures when you sing but I don't know where that comes from."

"No use asking because she don't know how she do it herself," the cornet man said, like somebody asked him to comment.

Cora lifted her eyebrows then turned back toward me. "He's right, Bessie. I listened until the music fit me."

"I don't understand."

She took a drag on a cigarette. "I sing what I mean and mean what I feel. If I feel happy, then that's how it sound. If I feel a rock against my head, then the music says that."

"Tell the truth, singers don't know nothing about music," the guitarist said.

The trumpet player looked up square and smiled. They were strong men, their instruments small against their bodies. The cornet player raised the horn's mouthpiece to his eye like a spyglass, his mind full of songs.

"Musicians think they invented music," Cora said, her hand on mine.

"Laugh if you want to, but singers don't know their notes," the horn player said.

"S'pose you do?" Cora said.

"Don't have to read music to know what I play."

"How's that different from me singing notes?" Cora said.

"It takes science to find my tone. Got to hurt yourself to make your lip tremble a tone. You can't just open your mouth and have something."

"You don't know what I do to sing. Your horn no better than my voice. Bessie, listen here. If they could sing, they would. They play that horn because they can't, but according to them I don't know anything."

Cora pinched my cheek and smiled. "Sure you want to do this?" she said.

The customers talked and drank. Slight creases formed at the corners of her eyes and mouth. She raised her hand toward the cornet player who lightly folded her fingers into a fist. I guessed by that it was time for me to leave.

* * *

46

Andrew thought he was a man after Clarence bought him snap front drawers and tight pants. He surprised me by insisting we work the riverside joints. We walked there when the last light sent the whores on duty.

"Let me do the talking," he said.

I followed him to a pier where splintered crates blocked alleys and dogs scavenged. A trolley bell echoed from downtown. Wagons, mules, and a few trucks clogged the street. Joints and saloons leaned like cards. The smell of chili blasted from a nearby joint. Greasy smoke hung in the doorway.

"Can you play that box?"

A man dealt cards to himself in a room barely lit by an oil lamp.

"What's the matter, never seen a white man in a nigger joint? Play something."

We ragged and danced the usual stuff.

"And you, big boy, what you do?"

"I'm her brother."

"Ain't that nice."

He looked at me funny from head to legs then all the way up again.

"Come closer so I can see you. You're younger than I thought but I need some noise. Thirty five cents a night and all the tips you can keep. If I find you're selling pussy and don't give me none, it's your balls," the man told Andrew like I wasn't even there.

"Your sister can really holler but she'll need a torch to be seen when the sun goes down," he said like he was cute.

"Fuck you, mister. Your mammy and daddy too," I said.

"Y'all sure some uppity niggers," he said.

I was out in the street in a second. The man laughed as Andrew scrambled after me.

47

"He didn't mean nothing, Bess. He offered us food and work."

"Who wants the man's rat tail gumbo? Did you hear what he said to me?"

"They all talk like that," Andrew said.

"Not to me, they ain't. Tired of hearing about my color."

We pushed each other around until I stepped away. Didn't hear nothing but street noise after that, sounds with no meaning that made me jumpy. I stole an apple off a cart. Andrew crossed to the other side of the street beating those strings the way he'd like to do me. He was a shadow going by, far as I was concerned.

I imagined the shoes, hats, and velveteen in the shop windows were mine. A young cloud of a woman tumbled from the doors, hands full of goods. Sweat washed my neck. The girl's hair was dark silk like the wig in the window, hair that would look better on me. I had just stepped off the big stairway at the end of the block when I heard my name whispered. Margie, her little brothers, and One Eye thought they couldn't be seen in the shadows under the stairs. It was a shame for them to play hooky and get babies drunk but I fell in with them. They let the youngest one drink from the jar lid and smile like a wino. I slapped One Eye every time he touched me. Bright planks of light opened and closed. We sat in the dirt, mocked the dull world above us. Who cared what Andrew or a fat-ass pimp wanted? A fruit seller saw me wobble up the steps to the sidewalk. She hawked berries with a howling soprano that time had made rough. She tried to warn me.

"Chattanooga ain't no dream," she said as I stumbled past.

They say I danced with my skirt above my knees, forced ofays off the sidewalk, marched in and out the big stores like I belonged there. Somewhere behind me, the fruit seller called my name. A white woman stepped in front of me then stopped like a mule. I tumbled into her.

"Get this nigger off me!" she said.

I got up but the sun blinded me. Trying to flatten a slanted sky caused me to knock over boxes of nails and tools stacked nearby. Hot iron nicked me. Hard dust clouded everything. A white son-of-a-bitch came swinging, lying about how I stole something so I took him down. His friends twisted my arms back like a chicken so the liar could hit me. I counted my teeth in the police wagon.

Into the drift, every breath gave half the air I needed. I remembered mistaking the cross weave of shadow and light from the sidewalk above our drinking club for steps to a street.

The jail had a cool mossy wall to press my life against. The men on the other side threw over notes and cigarettes like we were going someplace. I dreamed a road with thimble-sized trees. I didn't answer when Margie and the rest were dragged in. Her big mouth gave the cops my name.

I have heard for the rest of my life how Viola turned every corner in Chattanooga looking for the back of my head. She said downtown looked like nobody worked but her. Andrew gigged the whole night by himself, then was robbed on the way home.

Viola rocked in Mama's chair until morning to be at the cell door when the drunks were dragged in from the pier. They all shook like willow trees when the cops made them stand up straight. Nobody cared about the whites being drunk per se. Being a drunk nigger was all the difference. Viola put down five dollars and pleaded the judge to not send me to the pen. I asked Viola to not forgive me and there was no argument. She marched me to the back yard while neighbors giggled.

"Outhouse is where you belong."

She opened the privy door. I figured she'd set me free after while but she refused to let me out. Stink everywhere, I got nervous, lost my balance, slid in the hole, my butt too close to the mess. I sprung off the privy box and crashed the door so sweet it almost came off.

"Break it down and you'll shit in the street," Viola said, worry all in her voice. She must of unlatched the door the moment before I was gonna bust it down because I was outside so fast it's a blessing nobody got killed.

She and I were born of the same mama and papa, but think we cared? That's why spider webs got mixed in Viola's precious face cream years ago. Vengeance calms me down.

"Don't come back until you have my bail money," Vi said.

I ran to alcohol, came back without a penny. Viola said it was too bad there was only one life to hurt me in. Her blows brought no pain because I rocked a crib on high. It was 1910. I was fifteen with no man or baby to hold me, laughing because I had no sense.

⚞ Chapter 9 ⚟

Every day brought more electric lights and nickelodeons showing cars racing backward, motherfuckers barreling over Niagara Falls. We got a photo postcard that showed Clarence sitting on a paper moon. Behind him cardboard comets and stars hung from strings.

"Dear everybody, I'll be in at the Cavalcade Theater in May. Love, CS." I pressed that card against my lips and prayed.

"I suppose you won't do a lick of work until he comes," Viola said.

The day Clarence's show hit town, rain poured and poured. We were folding clothes when he came home.

"Don't hug me, peoples, I got my work clothes on," he said, dressed in a pleated shirt, box back coat, and tapered pants. Even Viola was impressed.

"You in love?" I asked.

"With myself." His eyes laughed. "All of y'all use your head. Tinnie, what you want for that baby? Viola, same question. Bessie, what you think?"

"I'm going to be rich."

"Knew I could depend on Bessie."

Viola's lips moved but nothing came out. When there was disagreeable work to be done he'd say, "Let the white folks do it."

When we were alone, I brought up Cora Fisher to show I was trying to better myself.

"You know about Ma Rainey?" Clarence said.

"Who's that?"

"Then you have no business going on the road with me."

My voice broke. Tears pooled up.

51

"We need a dancer."

"I can't leave right now. What's Viola gonna do?"

All those years arguing but I cared about her after all.

"I love Viola too but it's time for you to go," Clarence said. "Four o'clock. Tomorrow. Do your best better than it's ever been done. Work with me and we'll send some real money home to Viola and the babies."

I arrived at the Cavalcade sweaty and wrinkled. Nothing fit and taking clothes off and on again made me look worse. Nerves slipped a nine pound hammer in my shoes. Clarence linked his arm with mine.

"Bessie, this is Gertrude Rainey."

I played calm. Ma was little and low with haystack hair, a yellow sash around her forehead, shiny beads on her neck. Teeth framed in gold, rings on too many fingers, like she couldn't choose then decided to wear them all. A mess in other words.

"Pleased to meet you," she said.

She introduced the manager and two male dancers. The Cavalcade was half the size of the Ivory Theater. Seats almost on stage. The room felt crowded even when empty.

"Relax, follow the cue, do a time step and repeat it while we stretch out. That's it. We don't want nothing fancy," the horn player said.

I easily did what they asked.

"If she don't faint onstage, she can have it," the boss said.

"Don't you want to see nothing else?" I said.

Clarence cued me to shut up but I tossed my arms, drooped my mouth like rubber, crowd pleasing tricks that brought coin in the past. The happy feeling in the room ran out the door.

"You're good, but we want simple. Already got the leads. Sure you won't cause trouble?"

I swore I wouldn't but if I was a car they'd have kicked the tires. Clarence took me outside.

"Didn't you see me shake my head? When I give a signal, don't embarrass me. Understand?"

About ten minutes later Ma stood in the entry, arms open wide.

"Welcome to the show Bessie. Break both them pretty legs. This here is a try-out. No promises on anything. Twelve dollars for two weeks. You still willing?"

I left the audition on legs that could cross rivers, valleys lay at my feet. Already spent money I hadn't earned yet on imaginary clothes and a car. Saturday noon, two boys bannered the parade through downtown followed by the dancers who had auditioned me. They cakewalked the street on stilts followed by a brass band. A veiled woman's fat water snake passed for a python. It draped her shoulders while she sat on the wagon with Ma & Pa Rainey, who sang and joked while blackface clowns trotted behind them. That's what it took to pack the Cavalcade that night. The veiled lady oozed on stage with the snake hid in her costume. She swayed to a noisy house but the talking stopped when the serpent's head slid from up her sleeve. Some folk stood on chairs as the snake coiled her arms, around her breast. You should have heard the screams when she kissed the ugly thing right on its snout. Next came the "Cuban" acrobats that looked right black to me. The Singing Twins and the Bandana Dancers that got big applause but the show belonged to Pa, a string bean man with a crooning voice, and Ma.

I ain't got nobody but I want to be got by you.

Pa walked slowly to stage right then turned and fell on his butt. Drum rolls and horns squealed like a barnyard. He righted himself, fished a whistle from his pocket, blew hard but nothing came out. Disgusted, he pulled a handkerchief from his ear, farted through his nose, stretched the handkerchief to a point and out popped three paper flowers. Suddenly, a blue trumpet line. Ma swept in singin',

He's a fool, but I can't let him be

He don't do like he ought to

But somehow he satisfies me

Ma knew humor and pity. Her voice dark and low yet ringing, husky but clear. It pushed the thoughts of the listeners around. She greeted cheering tongues and yearning eyes, then settled into the moment.

I wake up early in the morning

'Fore the break of day

Said I wake up early, child,

Up for the break of day

I work hard for his breakfast

I struggle so he can play.

Front row, back row, what did she care, the whole room was hers. Threw her fat shoulders back, one hand waved time while the other invited us to the foot of her bed. She was sweet and tough, didn't wave a snake or balance on a wire. She talked about her fine shoes and how she'd rather go barefoot and we believed it. Seemed like she sang for a minute, that's how fast a long time went. People wouldn't let her go, kept making her encore until the manager said he was calling the sheriff if they didn't leave.

Ma hypnotized me. Viola dabbed her eye with the corner of her blouse.

"Why you cry?" I said. "This show made me happy."

"Bessie, that's where we're different. Her singing reminded me of Mama, of times that won't come no more."

"Black Patti was my favorite until tonight," I said.

"Don't tell me nothing about Black Patti. Don't call her name. Already lost Clarence because of people like her. Forget what I said about Ma Rainey, she's nothing but a whore." Viola's face locked, her eyes dimmed. "I'm not a child, Bessie, I know you're leaving."

She parted the crowd, her head cast down.

When Clarence came to say goodbye next morning, he expected me packed and ready. I saw him glance around for the clothes I'd stashed at the theater.

"You lose something?" Viola said, her eyes on both of us.

I sat on the bed, afraid to say what I'd planned. Andrew played all our songs on the porch, hoping we would take him too.

"Clarence, sorry to see you go. I worried you planned to take Bessie but now I got hope," Viola said.

Her voice turned almost happy. Clarence cleared his throat as he handed her twenty dollars.

"As a matter of fact..."

"Matter of fact, what? Don't even think about Bessie leaving. I can't do it all with just me, Tinnie, and Lulu. Bessie can't go," Viola said, the baby in her arms.

Clarence looked to me but I was no help.

"You're in heaven now, ain't you?" Viola said, mad because I could dream and she had forgot how. Her neck became a sunflower stem on its way out. She looked pretty in her sadness. When I promised to fill her pockets with enough gold to bring a headache, she cursed me out and set her baby howling. The house shrunk, sadness took hold. She threw Clarence's twenty dollars on the floor knowing he had to pick it up. Viola carried on like her baby was my fault. I knew everyone has a freedom to lose, but there wasn't a good way to say it.

The train left out about ten o'clock, headed south through the crop lands to Rome, Georgia, bound for Atlanta, booked into whistle stops like Shannon, Ball Ground, Calhoun, Fairmount, Lindale. I got bored on my first train ride, the chunk a chunk of wheels mile after mile.

Clarence tried to make me feel at home but I learned there was no home on the road, only the next place.

The colored rode in the baggage cars breathing smoke and dodging sparks. Up went the windows but stiff seats, heat, and bad air forced us to lower them down, then up and down again to breathe fresh and still escape the stink of dung. I never got used to it. Squeezed my legs together tight because it was a long ride between toilets and I wasn't squatting over a spittoon. Ma pinched my arm friendly when I asked for a mirror. The afternoon turned golden and clear. Wide flat fields all around the station.

We finally arrive in Rome, gathered around the manager hungry, tired, and got told we didn't have a place to stay.

"Sorry you come, ain't you?" Clarence said to me.

"Guess I thought..."

"Just some snow in July," Ma Rainey said, hooking her arm in mine. "I'm ready to make a pallet in a wagon track."

"Then you're saying that this ain't bad," I said, afraid her comment wasn't a joke.

"My name means something down here." Ma said.

About an hour later Pa and the manager returned, saying the rooming house wasn't far. The landlady was proud to have the Moses Stokes traveling show business, but worried.

"The sheriff don't want me successful and I don't give no suspicion to arrest me. I'm serious about no men creeping in your bed. I'll put you out in a minute."

"If I can't sleep with Ma, the other fellas won't neither," Pa said.

"You better hush up on me, Mr. Rainey, because you're free to go," Ma said.

Pa looked like he was going to get into it with her but changed his mind. Ma adjusted the rings on her left hand, smoothed her skirt, ready to pounce if he said another word.

At supper I gobbled tripe soup like it was rib eye. We turned in early on a bed lumpy as day-old grits. Closets held dusty clothes bundled with a curtain cord. Ma and I slept like sisters until I woke around 4 a.m. afraid I'd made a big mistake. Next morning Pa and the manager went to pick up the touring car and a truck, but the agent shook his head.

"I never rent to a nigra I don't know and ain't starting now."

"What's the problem? We used you last year," our manager said.

"No, boy, no. You ain't been here no last year. Was a white man who rented under Moses Stokes that time. I know Ma and Pa but they ain't the signatories."

"What you got then, sir? We got shows to do. We'll take a truck and a wagon. We got a lot of miles to cover."

"I got a two fine wagons and mules and that's all I can do under the circumstances. Take it or leave it."

The slow ride and the mule's butt made me sick. I threw up twice, had to piss in some high grass and bushes. Ma and Delilah told me to never piss by myself because there really were snakes sometime. I left steady work at home to come where nothing made sense.

"Spring planting's over, now's the time to shake nickels loose. Best shows are in the middle of a field with crickets knittin'. Nothing better than coal oil lamps on a traveling stage," Ma said.

Pa drove the mules saying nothing, his eyes focused like he could see past walls. The manager rattled off names of towns that weren't on any map.

"They all cracker towns," Pa said, like he'd never realized this before. "They mind their business if we do."

"Everybody love us long as we're singing," Ma said.

"They sure love a woman."

"Do tell," Ma said.

"You know what I mean," Pa said, "Never know who needs a convict for sixty days."

"Steal a woman or a man?" Ma said.

She turned full around direct in Pa's face.

"MAN, M-A-N, that's what I'm talking about. Stealing a man," Pa said.

"There you go again. That man stealing only happen one time I know for sure," Ma said.

"You forget I was a man when you were a child," Pa said, lowering his hat brim against the lazy heat.

"Yes sir. Was I your wife then?" Ma answered.

I was a beginner, too green to care about their troubles.

"Why we got to come way out here? Can't these folks to come to town like they do in Chattanooga?" I said.

"They're chained to the turpentine pines," Pa said.

"Don't men in Chattanooga get grabbed off the street?" Ma said.

"Sure", I said, wishing I'd paid better attention to the rest of the world.

"You might see some of them again out here," Ma said.

I pictured falling trees, brothers chained to roots flying free before they fell. The mule's harness clanked while we pitched and rolled the reddish hills. Views rose and changed, powder dust dripped from leaves.

"Comin' up on it," yelled the lead wagon when we finally reached New Hope Plantation. I saw a little drizzle of buildings, dark fields and sky, long rows of green shoots tended by stooped backs.

When our wagons pulled alongside, townsfolk raised their hats in welcome. Dark faces and homely clothes. Their children ran and leaped around us crying "Vagabons!" Three old women stood apart in the mud wringing sweat from their kerchiefs. They had seen foolishness like us before.

I thought we'd rest but the tent was up in two hours, entry wings folded back, tacked tight, the stage locked down and oil lamps set. My job was to hustle Red Hots, mammy dolls and peanuts from a tray roped around my neck. I wore a clown suit, my face painted black as a locomotive. Clarence drew white circles around my eyes and my mouth so I looked like a damn racehorse.

"What's this s'posed to show?" I said.

"That you're a convict trying to dance."

"All these people are black. Why we painted up way out here?" I said.

"Welcome to show business," he said.

Clarence had talked so much about cities filled with glamour and thrills. He didn't mention a sore butt caused by riding a creaking wagon or swallowing flies while you're hustling stale corn. I sucked my teeth and pretended I was on top of the world.

Slaw, the cornet player, and I sat together on the wagon.

"Drive this son of a bitch slow," he said to Pa. "Take it down so I can talk to these people. Bessie, get off and run along side." Slaw stood on the driver's seat and spieled the crowd followed by *Bill Bailey* played loud and hot while I shimmied against the beat, on my own and free.

"What's your name?," the workers asked.

"I'm Bessie Smith. That's B-E-S-S-I-E. Remember me."

We pulled the fields then out to the shacks and their nipping dogs, gourds hanging from bamboo poles. I forgot my hunger, charmed by the locals chanting my name.

A solid week of confusion with a group of hot, short tempered people. At afternoon break, Ma waved me behind a sheet tied between trees. She sat before a big collection of bottles and creams on a folding table, a silver mirror in her hand. She dusted her face with a light foundation that brought her skin several shades brighter.

"The world wants a light-skinned girl but I can touch them with my music. After that, being black don't matter. Fool 'em Bessie, and get what you want. Help me change." She pointed to a gauzy brassiere. "Fasten it on me."

She took off the blouse, cupped her breasts so the nipples peeped between her fingers. My mouth hung open. I gave her the brassiere. Her right breast filled the mirror she held. Ma leaned back until her spine rested on my hand.

"You okay?" Ma said as she rolled herself into the bra. "Four snaps, Bessie. You do it about well as Pa."

She stroked my hand from wrist to fingertips and palms. She wiped dust and sweat off my face, then smoothed the new crap on. Greased my hair until it rested light against my head. Each touch brought me closer to her. My breath changed to a purr.

I played my first show to a big crowd under a sky thick with stars. Every act was good but Ma set the night straight. Got blue from measure one because she was home. The sides of tent rolled up, shooting stars and blues falling down. I hummed while Ma turned the souls inside out. I was greedy for what she knew, the love that strangers gave. She didn't have nothing but the tumbledown life, teeth higglety-pigglety as a poor girl's fence. Sang about loving the dog tired man she married, how life was her own, her money snug against her ribs.

I got back to Rome, Georgia raw from skeeter bites, grateful to Ma for witch hazel and whiskey. She came to bed baby-talking, stroking my neck and shoulders. I almost said stop but I trusted her. Kept my eyes closed like a square while her fingers slid. I opened my mouth and let her tongue in, sank into softness and heat. She had me naked, her face between my thighs, my breasts smoothed and sucked. We rattled the bed in slow time, wet and rubbing hard until we got it. The next morning

60

Ma's hand danced between my thighs. I lay still, eyes wide, wanting her to explain, but instead of talking she stroked me again and again.

When we got through she sponged me with rose water, offered a new pair of panties. She made me wear them and nothing else. I hesitated but couldn't say no.

"Hours fly when you get what you want," she said. Barely breathing while summer light poured. Sharp voices just steps away. I raised up ready to lie if we were discovered.

"Door's locked, " Ma said, reading my mind. "Oo wee, baby. Now let me see some more."

She saw no flaws, all of me was beauty. The door rattled again. I stiffened, reached for my dress.

"Uh oh. I see Ma got a new one," a voice cooed from the hallway.

"We ain't saving food 'cause you already had breakfast."

When we got to the table the landlady looked like she knew. Ma didn't care a bit and that made me hot. We went back to the room. I stopped thinking before I spoke. My mouth went dry, my voice louder than it needed to be.

"I ain't funny, Ma. I hope you know that."

"You like a whole lot of love and smart enough to take it," she said.

"People call us freaks if they knew."

"People call too much."

"I can't be liking another woman. What will my brother think?"

"Can't, what you mean can"t? You already said I wasn't the first," her face right in mine. "I don't know what your brother thinks, Bessie."

I could tell she cared because her shoulders dipped, her eyes moist. She cradled my head between her palms, nose to nose.

"If your love come down, how you pretend it didn't?"

Ma showed concern but I wasn't used to it.

"I love you, Bessie."

She said it low and quiet and there was no shame in it.

"I want some air," was all I could say.

"Be pretty and get Ma some tobacco."

I walked around the town pouring smoke in no hurry to return. Houses built just a few yards from the tracks stored the dust thrown by the trains under porches and against fences. Bushes and trees bent weird by rushing wind. Houses fluttered when a freight rolled past. Nothing to remember here except a clock tower in the distance, Ma's coarse tongue, her peppermint teeth.

Hometown faces stared like they knew me but didn't ask. Plenty my color, deep browns to pure "b" black, tall women with dumpling breasts and cheeks. I didn't encourage their hot-eyed men and not responsible for hopes they had.

* * *

There wasn't much to do between shows but every now and then something would crop up.

"Why are we stopping, Ma?"

"Cause I want a picture by the plantation."

"Why?"

"Some of my people slaved here."

"Why remember that?" I said.

"Cause I want to."

"Your mouth will look funny in the picture."

"Shut up."

"Lean up beside that column and straighten your tie. Do it for me, baby."

"You posing mighty mannish," I said.

"Is that a compliment or a complaint?" Ma said.

"What you think?"

"I don't care myself."

"It was a compliment," I said.

"That's better," Ma said.

Clarence knew what was what between Ma and me but let me fend for myself. The river rode flat and high nearby. Next afternoon, we crossed a bridge onto a wide levee. Two white men with shotguns waved us toward two black men on horses who cradled whips while zebra suit convicts found rhythms to shovel mud and sand. You'd thought the Kingdom had come by the way convicts shouted "Ma's back, Ma's back!" A bit farther on we found tents, metal cages tall as a man, and a big log shed .

"That's the playhouse," Ma said.

It was nothing much. The floors looked like whatever fell stayed for a long time. A tin roof, no windows. Ma gave a look to settle me down. The boss man kept a jar of teeth on the bar for good luck, but said he didn't pick up nothing else.

"Let's talk dollars," Ma said.

"The sheriff will brew hell if there's trouble," the boss man said.

"You know what will happen if I don't get paid," Ma said.

"Already shot three of 'em this month but they love you, Ma. Look forward to you..."

"I want my money."

When Ma returned from the boss' office she pulled me aside.

"We sing by the door, but we don't run."

"This is place is filthy," I said.

"You'll forget it when lights are low. Always pray you will see the end of a show. Second thing is never tease men in a swamp"

"What?"

"Slap their hand before they find your water and never come between a man and his boy-gal.

"They allow that?"

"Oh Lord. Better stay close to Ma."

Years later, we'd laugh about this while playing for the same girl. I usually said "Go 'head Ma, you got the best strokes." I never lived with a woman but it was so comfortable to be girls together, wild and smoky, free from a grinding man.

After several weeks it looked like I'd earned my keep. We'd changed from mules to trains, cars, and an old bus. It all felt regular by then, like the world I hoped for when I was begging on the streets with Andrew. One night Ma dragged out her entrance so long, the crowd lost patience with me and the other hoofers stalling for time. Folks left their seats hollering for Ma, catcalling, throwing stuff. To protect myself, I stepped out of the dance line toward the footlights, talking about,

> See See Rider,
> See what you done done...

Clarence tried to escort me off stage but I wouldn't go. He tried telling jokes but I had it red hot and he couldn't upstage me.

"Boy, get off the stage and let that gal sing," someone said.

Did he think I was a tree to pee on? I was helping Ma out. I preached them people until it was a shame. Pa stroked his banjo down low like milking a cow. He jerked like a fish on the line and made the tent quiver. I had five different men walking to the stage, folding money in their hand.

See See Rider
You made me love you
Now your man have come.
Careless love,
See what you have done.
I won't be blue always

Bracelets and brown eyes, a big sex desire, forgetting all consequences, only the holding close to another came tumbling from my mouth blue streaming down. Ma Rainey probably watched a long time before signaling me to get off stage. She rumbled her boyfriend voice and I should have begged her pardon but I dreamed we were equals because the crowd seemed to like me. All of Ma's necklaces shook when she took the stage and showed me what was what. From then on she didn't look my way, and nobody noticed when I baby-stepped off. It was a whole day before Ma took me back. She didn't preach and I didn't act up. I drank her cool water and dreamed a heaven of my own. There were no tornado-sized arguments with Ma; she just told me I wasn't cut out to be her assistant. I was my own deal.

"You got to prove yourself up and down this highway like I did. Flat as a suitcase, hot as a fire, it's your front room and kitchen from now on," she said.

Ma didn't leave me by the train tracks like she could have. Wasn't nothing Clarence could do if she had. Through her I found out the Cotton Blossoms needed a dancer and said goodbye to the best performer I'd ever seen. Even worse, one day I'd have to compete with her. I tried to remember lessons she'd preached, the cunning her slow jive disguised.

Rule One: You ain't a whore until you decide to be. Two: Never let a manager keep your money in a safe. Three: Ship your trunk even if you have to walk.

"Why are you so ignorant, Bessie?" My brother's words tumbled out.

"The crowd was with me and I couldn't stop."

"You mean wouldn't stop. The crowd has gone home and what have you proved?"

"I didn't think about that."

"You could go back to Chattanooga and listen to Viola say 'Told you so' 'til you kill her."

He threw a soft punch then hugged goodbye. I'm a fool sometimes. Threw away a good job because I forgot who the star was. Much as Ma liked me, she could always kiss another if I didn't work out.

ᛉ Chapter 10 ᛃ

I rode the Blossoms far as I could milk it. It was steady squares for eight dollars a week. Ma had tried to grease the skids by saying I was "the best she'd seen in a great while" but the manager did everything but make me strip like a slave. I even walked up stairs with a basket on my head.

"Well?" I said.

"Don't say anything, Miss. I'm seeing you onstage. Just have patience."

He signed me on Ma's recommendation. If I'd argued, he'd have dropped me. I expected to be treated like a beginner and was not disappointed. The Cotton Blossoms didn't baby anyone but the manager's favorite. I loved her clothes, especially the lace-up shoes that were pure money. Politeness and glad-handing disappeared a few miles down the track.

"Get up out of my seat. Don't get in my place again," she said.

"How could I know the seat was yours if it was empty when I came in?"

"If you're not sure, ask. I always sit by the window opposite the sun. Don't sit with me unless I invite you. Don't hold your breath."

"That's all right," I said through tight lips and vowed to take her job. I moved to another row and let that train put me in a different town. To keep my spirits up, I sang my favorite Ma Rainey tunes. If the manager happened by, I'd let the sound get big. He stopped to listen about a week after hiring me.

"Bessie, I don't need another singer. Get that through your mind. I need a clown, a dancer, a errand-runner. I don't want that Ma Rainey moan here, we go for a high tone show."

He had to remind me I was the blackest thing on the dance line, but think I cared what he thought? Black as he was, thinking yellow was the only color worth having? The musicians gave me some interest but I wasn't playing merry-go-round. I followed the other females to a lodging house but they snatched the good beds before I had a chance. The maple-skinned star wasn't but two years ahead of me. She had good moves but her sound was wiry and tight. I was a willow tree with flowing leaves in a straight black dress. Stage lights loved my sweat. When there was work to be done I didn't try to hide. Wasn't long until we had taken in stranded show-folk hustling courtesy meals. I listened to their swindled tales and knew their trouble could be mine overnight.

I caught a break when the lead singer caught the croup. The other girls thought they had a chance until I took a verse. The manager told me not to get used to her spot but his headliner looked worried when she realized I had memorized her act. In Greensboro, we performed in a converted barn, one of those halls where sound dribbled out like air from a slow leak. When the country folk gaggled in, their lonely mouths telling tales, even the brass got buried. The star jumped hard on the beat but her toy voice whimpered across the front rows. The locals said, "Start the music, we here to dance." The girl lost her voice again trying to fill what she wasn't built for.

"Bessie, take it," the manager growled.

She huddled in his arms, every muscle hating me. I didn't try to sing high, just found the loudest tones and pushed them hard. The crowd swam in the music like they were being paid for surviving. When we closed hours later, I hoped for a featured place. Waited for compliments that didn't come. The singer let down her meanness, thanked me, even suggested singing louder since my voice was so strong. I thought, "You think I'll blow up just in time for you to take over but I'm a loudmouth that don't wear out. I drink from a secret well." Ma Rainey herself couldn't have gotten more down in the alley. That show made the cornet player nurse his lip for days. The crowd lifted up like they'd been freed and made safe. The show went so well, I let myself forget that the sign out front said "Tan Beauties."

"Thanks, sweetheart, good work," the manager said, but he never let me front the show again.

"My name's Bessie Smith, I'll dazzle your eyes and bless your ears," was my intro. It does no good to give a great show if nobody knows who you are. The manager might not want me out front, but audiences did. I gave encouragement to the knock-kneed girl who thought I was already famous, smeared a touch of soot on a boy's nose, scrawled my name on church fans. Their admiration was a blessing.

My latest best friend found a saxophone player with an extra ticket to Chicago. We hugged kiss-kiss goodbye when she gave me her old coat. Alone again, I hoped for a new companion who was clean and wouldn't steal too much. I rode high for a good while but got stranded again. Everybody but the manager and the trick star walked track back to Bessemer, Alabama. I had five dollars and lots of daylight ahead. The show had ditched us and there was no use crying now. Walked between the tracks, hot nails for stones. A girl walked up the embankment to meet us.

"It's August and there's no Mama to run to. My hands are filled with raw cotton. It sticks to my palms and my fingers are caught in the boll. Hard little hooks fasten my skin. They had to cut my fingers free," she said.

I listened to the noise in her voice. It was a howling fire but her head hung down. A shadow could have pushed her around. Bare toes jammed back to her feet caused a stumbling gait. Her skin was permanently sanded by the gray earth. She was dark skinned but she had faded. I was going to hustle a meal from her until I saw her luck was worse than mine. I gave her a long blue dress from my grip just to show concern. I left her calling after me, thanking me for something I could have thrown away in a wild moment.

I was motherless and jobless but I wasn't picking cotton. We all walked toward the sun. The two horn players said there was too many of us together. The musicians said it was more dangerous to be too few. Viola had prophesied I was going to miss her one day, going to pray I was back on Ninth Street singing:

Left and Juber Right – Juber dance with all your might.

I guess Viola knew more than I thought.

❦ Chapter 11 ❧

Good thing the promoters believed I was too dark to be the star; it gave me room to learn. I watched the theater-owners cull the curly-head light, bright ones, dazzle young stupids into taking off their hand me downs and stepping into cheap half-silk behind the stage. I knew where they were headed even if the show hit the boards. Watched them play a dancer off the singer then drop them both in a saloon in East Hell where their legs would never close.

I did everything from blacking up to play a man, to clowning with a red nose and elephant shoes, but I couldn't let the rain run cold down my back while I begged strangers for a way home. Hunger, my judge and witness, was never far away. Maybe my size kept the trouble down. I stood five foot ten and didn't slouch. I had so much energy the bookers hired me to do two people's jobs.

I danced, shimmied and shuffled, ragged and two-stepped, slid on my butt, swung from a rope, held the net for the girl shot from the cannon. Worked circus, coon show, vaudeville and private party. I bought clothes when people died, could style hair and not burn it up. I learned that pearls matched my teeth and gold was my favorite color. Booking agents sent me to the cotton country because I wouldn't come back crying. The farmers left their hidden towns to juke when the crops were barely laid in. I fell into their crossroads and learned the licks that kept them dancing. Nothing there but the cool evening behind the sun, all pain forgotten until the night was hoarse and dry.

I told this girl who was impressed with me, "If I could sing like a rabbit fucks, everything will be mine. That bridge is too ugly for me. I want the grand hotel. There won't be nothing but black folks in it and all of them will know I'm queen." If her mouth stayed open too long I'd put my tongue in it and make promises I couldn't keep.

By 1914, I'd had years of twenty dollar a week gigs. I was hired for my reputation as an all-round talent and worth a lot more.

"One day you won't be able to afford me, but you'll pay it anyway,"

I warned the stingy managers, the same ones who would pay top dollar
plus a hundred when I made my name. They buried me in the dance line
in the big shows, a cardboard cutout of flower petals around my ears,
black grease oozing down my back. I experimented by mixing slick black
with sparkly sand. When the lights hit right, the reflection off the gloss
went gold like a miracle and the money came flying on the stage. I played
many a town saying "Real Colored Coon Shouters! Candy-lipped Gold
Dust Twins." I don't apologize for wearing the bandana with twenty
knots, pillows front and back draped with a checkerboard apron. Stepping
high, landing splits, we spread the black satin mess smooth, sealed wrin-
kles and bones to faces that were original and different until the grease
turned us all the same. We didn't give blackface a second minute because
it was common as greed. I was gonna have my dinner even if you didn't
invite me to yours. I kept count of the skimpy food days like some people
remember sleepless nights and made up for meals lost the week before.
I got fat on purpose and not full yet. Being poor was a problem, but fuck
crying.

Got tired of being the best thing on stage but never singing lead.
I married Earl Love in Mississippi because his voice was syrup.
It creamed over me and caused slow dreams. I stopped singing and
only used my mouth for pleasure, forgot about turning expressions into
songs, was through hooking trumpets to memories, telling no-counts
I loved them. I cut bait by the pond and dreamed about babies but didn't
tell my family about the marriage because I wanted to surprise them.
His people lived around an all black town, the place he called "a little bit
of heaven, folded between a creek and a high pasture."

The summer was sweet as pie but I was no good in the rain. Didn't
know planting or animals. This wasn't news, but it finally meant something. I was useless to them except for cooking but Earl stood with me.
I finally woke up singing and his people warned him about me.

"Earl, let's go to town and be young," I said, but it was bad for him.
Even tried to take him to Chattanooga to get away from the back biting.

"What time you got?"

"Middle of the night. Girl, go back to sleep."

"Earl, I want a piano."

"Don't you never rest?"

I tried to be silent after I got up. Covered my mouth then sang into the palms of my hands to enjoy my voice in private. I don't know how the dogs heard me over the racket crickets made.

"Bess, stop making them dogs bark. Come back to bed, I know what you want."

"I don't want that now. I hear a song but need a piano to get it."

"Sing in my ear, your tongue my drum."

"You'll be deaf 'fore I'm through. Songs slip away. They come so quick. All there, then gone."

"You're crazy. Always be another after that."

"No. Not true. Songs die like we do. This is calling me."

"Calling you?"

"Don't you understand nothing?"

"And you do?"

"If you get a letter, don't you want to read it?"

"Forget it, Bess."

"I already forgot it so many times because I love you. There's pianos everywhere but here."

Earl pried my hands from my eyes.

"Why you say 'yes' when I offered you a quiet life? Huh, why you say what you don't mean. I love you so much I want you close. I don't want you far away, a name in the paper somewhere."

I couldn't make him change any more than he could change me. The sky was close. Insects and breezes snapped into life. There were no years on his face. He didn't even know half my story, his hand folded across my heart. I leaned into the blues. I knew his people expected a baby by now and so did we. I would have gone to a doctor but he was real patient.

"I'm happy, baby, why ain't you? You love someone else?" he said.

"I love 'something' not 'someone'." I brushed his face with the back of my right hand. Slight mist rose off the pond, wild cricket music, the dark leaves and livestock sounds.

"Sing here all you want," he said. I could feel his tender bones just by looking at him but I uncorked my careless mouth and told him only he mattered. If he was in jail, I'd come there too.

"You'd do time with me?"

He wouldn't let me exaggerate. His hands were swollen from the plow I'd failed to master. I shook my fingers like they were wet.

"Yes, I'd do the time if I could."

"Could," says you don't mean it.

"'Could' means things come up and don't tease me about love," I said.

He let it go but his eyes searched for more weakness in me.

"Don't do it," I warned because he was looking for stains that didn't matter.

"People shouldn't make promises they don't mean," he said.

I wondered why a few out-of-place comments could make so much difference. His eyes welled with too many thoughts. A glowing trail of ants flooded the tree root beside us. I wanted our words to follow the ants into the silence, wondered if love really existed as I spread his fingers one by one. A train howled. He brought me close, my faults forgiven. I looked at my watch. He pointed across the night to the jerky light of the locomotive.

"Trains carry blues," he said with a wave of his hand. His people went into their low roofed house of chores and let us be.

"Why can't you compromise, Bessie? Your mouth is hard and selfish. How does the song come out?"

A country juke brought my marriage down. He forbid me to sing in the tavern but I had to. I promised Earl that I wouldn't disrespect him but the songs were choking me and I had to spit them out. Bargained that I could sing close to home and be satisfied, but he couldn't stand the thought of men loose in the same night with me. Didn't understand why I had to have my own money, why I had to make a stranger say my name.

Earl, me, and his people made it to the juke so I could get it out of my system. There was a pretty good bugle player and a wash tub bass. I fell into my routine and pretty soon my sound was too big for the room.

"Let's take it outside," the bass thumper said. "Out there you can holler all you want."

The echo from the creek sounded so good Earl's people tapped their feet but still planted trouble. He and I argued until love blew up. We agreed to have the preacher blot our names from the Marriage book. There wasn't a word of anger between Earl and me, only the scar fire leaves on your tongue. His people and I hardly spoke afterward. Their eyes showed sympathy but their smiles gave it away.

"Earl, I asked Papa Love drop me at the station instead of you. It's harder this way. We'll just go round and round about why I got to go and end up even more sad," I said.

"Then why did you get in the car with me?"

"Because I hoped we could get some understanding. You're the one who told your daddy that you were going to take me."

"Maybe you can drop me off like a cab fare but I can't do you like that. Start over with me, Bessie. Nobody says we can't get married and bust up every other week."

"That proves what?"

"I'm crazy about you."

"Then come see me when we don't have to promise anything."

"See, see right there, that's the difference between us, Bessie. Love won't mean nothing without a promise. 'Love' is my last name. Think I can sign it all my life and not think about what 'love' supposed to mean?"

"Count these tears, Earl. It ain't about loving or not loving. It's about me and a stage and what you can't allow. I tried here. Why can't you try the town awhile? You know I love you. I'm not leaving because I want to and you know it. Here come the train just when we're talking straight."

"I told you that train was nothing but the blues when we saw it go by from the farm. Now you got to git on and ride."

"Promise you'll visit, baby. Take this train with me. Don't just be saying nothing. Earl...?"

I cried about the letters that brought no reply. Mama always said the only blessing a colored woman had was a good black man and I'd let a good one go.

"What world you think this is, Bessie? Leaving a good man for a stage show? Have you lost your mind?" is what she would have said. The only fair answer is, "Yes, Mama, I've lost my mind."

Chapter 12

If Chattanooga was my idea of big city, then Atlanta in 1918 was two times that. Atlanta Negroes didn't hold back. Clothes? Top hats, full morning coats common to doctors and pimps alike. Indoor toilets, electric lights inside and out, life that I mostly knew from cakewalk promenades. Millionaires, black banks and hospitals, black police, all my world to a ragtime beat. Rhythm made Sweet Auburn sway. Didn't need Christmas to serve trombones for dinner, cornets for dessert, sugar oozing out.

I threw myself into backyard cattle calls at the 81 Theater and wouldn't believe a "No." All of us who wanted something besides the usual nigger-work had to get on stage and stay there. I gave up Mr. Love to sing so failing was not possible. The manager got sick of me real quick.

"Bessie, I said there was nothing for you. Now why you still here?"

"Cause my day will come."

"Can't take 'no' for an answer?"

"What you think?" I said.

I broke through by using the Eighty-One's rehearsal yard like curbstone in Chattanooga. Sang so loud the manager eventually couldn't stand it.

"Dammit girl, shut up that mouth and come on in. Maybe that noise means something."

I outworked everyone, never complained about long rehearsals and bad conditions. They paid ten dollars a week at first, half what I made before my marriage. When Ma Rainey saw me a few months later at 81, I was almost soft shoe slick. The band was tight. Only had sixteen bars on my own, but I made them count. Georgia Tom Dorsey had stopped hustling popcorn and was bending the piano keys when he told me to tone it down so he could hear his baby call. I told him to fix it himself then turned my big noise loose.

It took months at the 81 before Mr. Bailey offered me out-of-town gigs.

"It's big step up, Bessie."

"I want $40 a week guaranteed." I didn't blink, stayed in his face like a man. He faltered, that lip twitched. "I'll need three dancers, a magic act, two horns, and a git box."

"For all of you?"

"For me."

"Who you think you are, Bessie?"

"I'm the one people will come to see."

"I'll advance you $40 against sales. That's a loan, not a gift. Here's a list of theaters and itinerary. They will report their ticket sales to me. I'll book the first date but after that it's up to you. If the show dies, get your ass back here."

"You trust me with $40?"

"I'll get it back or you can kiss your career goodbye."

I spent two months crawling through Georgia, Alabama, and "Sippi" doing turn away business. We played every mole hill that said "hello." Rolled into towns the week after a lynching. Signs said "Nigger Don't Let the Sun Set On You," although most times the sheriff said, "Naw, that sign don't mean y'all, it's for them other niggers." Years later, the rainbow rained gold because of those days.

Brought those memories to Atlanta, straight to Decatur Street, bluer than when we left. Got promoted, made the 91 Club remember where folk plow half of hell to roll in juke joint aisles.

"Pick up on the blue. Play like Friday might not come," made the fancy players testify instead of think. Finally graduated to the "Toby Time," shorthand for Tough On Black Asses - Theater Owners Booking Association - the big city circuit for colored talent. I was second billed but onstage for a full thirty minutes and could hardly carry all the money

78

thrown at my feet. Went home Christmas and threw success around. I bought everyone new clothes and told Viola to stop crying.

"Life looks different when the money's long," I told Lulu, little sister no more. Her new purse and stockings matched the ribbons in her daughter's hair. They thought we were dreaming. I tried to talk Andrew into picking up his box but he had a woman, family, steady job as a jailer.

"C'mon brother, you and me again. The money is getting big."

"Go ahead Bessie, I'm small time but satisfied."

"This all you want, brother? What about all those dreams living good, living free?"

"I loves this girl, Bessie. She's from around here and don't like me to travel. I'm sticking with the jail. Go on and get what you want. I'm all for you."

* * *

I understood that spirituals, sanctified, ragtime, blues got mashed together and the music was the best it had ever been. Negroes carried a tune that didn't go stale. Life broke our heart yet we laughed. In King Oliver, a secret harmony was born. The horns told what the musicians thought and all else they desired. Enjoyed many a romance because I knew what the trumpeter's tongue said to the mouthpiece.

"You sure look good, Bessie. If that dress got any shorter, might as well leave it at home," they'd holler, hoping I'd be interested.

"You'd like that, I know."

"I can take it or leave it."

"Then why you lookin'?"

The tuba hits one and three, the banjo hard two and four, but the lift came from horns landing on *dit-dah-da-blip* and bam! Piano triplets, the quartet harmonizing *Love Me* five different ways into the early late.

I'd moved up in the touring world but got careless. Woke up by the

79

rooming house manager saying "pay the rent or go to jail." The booking agent had folded the show and left the performers holding the bill. Stuck in Birmingham, no show coming for a month, I saw a "help wanted" sign at a laundry and went back to slaving. Didn't matter this time, though. My name was out there, only needed to wait for the next show to come through.

One day a smooth youngster left a pile of fine clothes to be washed.

"You're new," he said.

"Yes sir, that's three dollars."

"What you doing here?" he said.

"I press and fold."

"No, baby, you don't belong here. Not with those fingernails and earrings."

"Nobody else even noticed."

"I'm different. My name is Richard Morgan and I'm somebody."

"Yes, you are," I said, leaning back to let my assets do the rest.

I knew he was young but so slick he passed for twenty; a lanky brown skin who belonged to somebody else and didn't expect to stay the night. We met just once more because I'd found a new show. He made me sing *Baby Won't You Please Come Home*, while he lay between my legs.

"You are the greatest ever," he said.

"Yes I am," I agreed.

* * *

By year's end I didn't hope for a part in somebody else's show, I wanted my own deal. My top was too busty, my backend was trouble, but my dance steps were tireless. I'd never be a kewpie doll and my complexion was too rich for managers to prize, but I knew I could win. I was tall as most men and they weren't getting if I wasn't giving. Girls on the road

80

had to stick tight or be eaten by the prowling manager and his running buddy, the wild dog pimp. We slammed doors on wolf paws from Baltimore to Mobile.

Me and Half-Pint Jaxon teamed for strict business, two pros working the hell out of a room. Teaming up let me develop a look and style that was different from anybody else on the scene. I'd learned to send my voice any place the song wanted to go. Every act had just a few seconds before shit got thrown at the stage. We learned the eye was more forgiving than the voice. If we introduced the new and sassy, the crowd was ready to try it on. I popped jokes while he razzle dazzled. "Don't miss this," Half Pint's cue for a double flip landed on the down beat, always rained cash on the stage. Fortune came because I had the moment in my heart.

Chapter 13

My movements were guaranteed. There was no bargaining with my certainty for everything. A rumor about me sent a Mr. Walker to catch my show in Selma, Alabama. He came early before the white show and sat in the back like a Yankee. I knew he was auditioning me for a record company. My lungs were wet smoke. It was the third show, still two to go. Even the tables were alive. I had locked the musicians to my plan. Bookies, shine boys, fortune tellers all looked my way. If I broke my shoe somebody would run to fix it. I hired boys to shout "Bessie! 81 Club, 9, 10:30, midnight and 2 a.m." Every seat filled.

Walker said I was the "real thing" but Columbia Records wasn't ready to take me yet. I didn't say anything while my fingers counted pearls. I winked at a used-to-be and wondered why this white man was wasting my time. Walker said he knew the "real Negro" sound, didn't say nigger or coon. Talked low, his words nearly secrets. Mamie Smith's *Crazy Blues* changed everything. Behind that, the record companies found out even the colored had a few dimes and "race" records started coming fast. Ma Rainey should have had the first blues out, but if you're waiting for fairness, you got to expect the sadness.

Mr. Walker was lucky my period was over and I was able to remember patience. Life on the Toby Time balanced between rumors and hope. Stale beer and secret kisses was our stock exchange. I had laced tears into songs and knew my value. All my jewelry had a story. The white man was sweating in a cold room that belonged to me. I guessed he was lonely for some more of his people but he'd be safe unless the cops came through. Walker stood near the door in case foolishness broke loose. A year ago the grapevine said a big-time man was asking for me but who's going to count on that? I was dressed nice for back then though I was too thin. My jazz babies flapped and stepped like rain. When they bent over, everybody stood.

I sat in Walker's car out front after the show. He showed me a heavy recording plate and said the world would go electric. Told how he'd sat on porches and in sweaty rooms across Georgia but never heard a sound like mine.

"I'm ready to record right there in the street," I said.

He changed the subject and asked if my bracelet was real gold. I scratched it to prove my value and asked him to open the car door so the world couldn't gossip.

"I don't worry about what people think," he said.

"Mr. Walker, if you own Columbia Records, why don't you make a deal right now?"

"I don't own it. I'm a worker like you."

He needed a recording to convince the big people in New York. He handed me a paper I wasn't gonna sign unless there was money up front. "Give me some more time, Bessie. Think of me as a friend. It will take time, but I'll come back."

"When, Mr. Walker? I don't stay here all year."

"You travel, I know."

"Uh-huh, I don't belong no one place but Atlanta."

"And Chattanooga?"

"Chattanooga is home but it don't keep me working. I'm a gal that stays hungry."

"You're still thin, though."

"Not for long if I got anything to say on it."

"Love the food, huh?"

"That's right, Mister. I don't miss a meal."

I told him to send the owner next time and left him sweating on the tough street. Wasn't nothing to do but stroke shine boy's head for good luck, breathe some good old sooty air. Tamale Man sold me one red hot. The thought that Mamie Smith had it first with her mashed potato moans! She was light skinned, but she'll grab a breath when I hit a step.

I was working Philly when W.C. Handy's company called me for a New York audition. Black Swan had already made some dollars off ragtime records. I told you those record companies had got hep to the "race" music trend. Maybe they heard the rumor Thomas Edison was interested in me. All I know is that I broke those scientists at Black Swan down with the blues. We recorded in a lab like Frankenstein's. They wore white coats and made machinery lights glow and jump. Hard to find harmonies when Percy's piano was half a room away. Mr. Somebody said to spit out my gum and not sneeze. The microphone was a glass flower and I had to sing one direction and not pat my feet. When I opened up, they stepped back like a storm was near.

"Awfully raw," they whispered. I wore real pearls and no whiskey breath. I told them I wasn't an opera singer. They give me little pit-pat applause after five takes like I was a spider in their tea. I mentioned Black Patti in case she was good enough for them. They played some recordings for me. They were slick and smart and I realized they only wanted some high class stuff that don't moan. I declared Ma Rainey was the Songbird of the South, but when they said New York winters were cold, I sure wished I had a pound of dirty chitlins to drop on their shiny floor.

New Orleans 1924 is where I fell for Sydney Bechet's swooping clarinet. He changed notes into fluttering birds and spoke like poetry. Bechet got famous early because there was nothing like him.

"Bessie, your voice is so blue it's calling the planets to come home. Only problem is that they won't land unless I'm in the band," he said.

"You moo like a calf crying for that butter and cream."

"That's alright Bessie, I love your butter because I'm full of cream."

"I hear you talking but it makes no sense" was my comeback.

"No baby, I am here to rescue you from ideas of animal husbandry, knowledge of crops, and labor you and I are not suited for."

"Bechet, you're a mess," I teased.

"My intentions are serious, honorable and inevitable."

"No, they're not. I know what you want."

"Then let's not waste no time. Don't you smell last night's gutters? Those oysters were alive six hours ago."

Bechet wasn't really my style. A lot of breast meat when I prefer the thigh.

"Don't assume the outer is my essence, Bessie. My granny was black as Africa although my skin was blended to the high cream of survival. Don't be impressed by my Creole manners. I've put a many a rounder through a parquet door."

"Bechet is more a sound than a name," I teased.

"These deadly avenues were my cradle, citified swamps where haints disguised as physicians nursed me among herons and reptiles. Names are useless in a haunted bayou pretending to be a town. Only talent is important."

Bechet put his arms around me and I wasn't disappointed by the time morning came.

"You're a genius and so am I," he said.

"Why you talk so much?"

"I can't imagine in silence like you."

We did some shows that should have been recorded. Best of all was listening to him rave about himself.

"C'mon Bessie, admit you love me."

"Bechet, you are two steps from Paris and New York and I'm still looking for a record date."

"Come to Paris and miracles will be an everyday thing. Haven't I proved that I can say 'motherfucker' like an eighth note tied across the bar?"

"Bechet, play your break. I'm booked again for Toby Time and got to go."

He knew I meant it. Rented a carriage, sang to me while I played it cool.

> *She's a silver horn in a crushed velvet case.*
> *She's tailor made,*
> *Ain't no hand me down.*

There was water in his eyes. Maybe he meant it after all.

I came back to the 91 in Atlanta and faked my cool. I was booked until Christmas, had three big rooms downtown, a bed like a river, two New Orleans mirrors and a card table for ten. Sent fifteen dollars a month to Viola and lacked for nothing but that feeling called love.

Jack Gee and Bessie

⚔ **Chapter 14** ⚖

The Toby Time booked me out of the Deep South with gigs in Chicago, Baltimore, New York. I liked Philly because it was smaller and cheaper than Harlem. There was a rail line straight up the Jersey shore to Atlantic City, a black scene that felt down home. I never imagined a pier big enough to be a highway. Clubs wide open at sunrise. Every hustle and sham already there or getting born. Atlantic City in 1920 was a swell good time but soon as September hit, black birds better sweep our straw and git. A gambler's heaven, a pimp's paradise, I worked four or five shows a night, hardly slept, but the young don't need sleep any more than they need to be sober. I found my crowd and learned to dress "East." Got introduced to chemise and bagels, northern bootleg and "sealed" liquor, though coupons on the bottles didn't mean shit since Prohibition freed the squares from rules. Flappers had no shame. They spun and flipped their dresses up to show it all and nobody cared. I poured brew and wondered on the tides under a sharp summer moon.

A man sat close to the stage as possible all five shows Sunday night; did the same thing several weeks in a row. He looked good from every direction but I made him wait. First came cards complimenting my dancing and singing. After he was sure I noticed him, the beating around the bush ended.

"Waiting for someone?"

"Maybe."

"Could I get you something to drink, Miss Smith?"

"No thanks."

"Live 'round here?"

"Uh huh."

"Miss Smith, you are the prettiest girl in here. I'm Jack Gee, private detective."

"A Do Right boy?"

"You don't remember me, do you?"

"From where?"

"Horan's, Philly. You were with friends."

"Could have been. I like to have my fun."

"So I noticed," he said.

Jack Gee was like a New Year: it appears out of nothing and suddenly it's all there is.

"Your voice has something I can't place," he said. I appreciated hearing that my voice couldn't be described.

"Kind of mysterious."

"Like something you forgot?"

His eyes locked mine, his laugh like thunder.

"You have a way with words," I said.

He leaned back to swallow, his face was pure, dark and new.

"What do you think about when you're singing?"

Few customers ever talked like this. He didn't ask about the songs, the steps I cut, or who I knew. I wondered why his question made me nervous. My voice was all I'd been but I didn't tell him that. It was too much mine.

"Must be mighty nice to open your mouth and that sound come ringing."

I didn't know how if this was a high-class compliment or the raving of a devil. We stayed together fifteen hours on our first night out. My show closed at 3 am and left plenty of time to hit the joints. Jack was ready to hit the sheets but I wouldn't fall that fast. My favorite bootlegger set up shot glasses across the bar for a tasting session. Jack got wobbly quick but I downed six or seven and felt good with it. He woke about 6 a.m. when I stroked his ears. Time we got to the room, we fell out fully dressed on the bed wondering how the world got so bright.

"You're pretty good for a copper. Sure you can keep up with me?"

"I'm all the way in," he said. I almost let him have it right then but decided to tone down my party girl habits because it looked like both of us were looking for something beside the usual. We exchanged numbers before I took the train back to Philly and got ready for the fall tours down south. For the first time in a long while, a man's voice stayed with me all the way home.

Back in Philly, me and Jack made a date, said the nervous words people use when they're getting serious about each other. I forgot my purse. Ran back for it, couldn't find my key, little delays that I should have listened to. Jack knew a shortcut to the restaurant. Soon as we crossed the street, voices were both ahead and behind us. Blam! Blam! Glass shattered without a sound. I thought this was a good neighborhood. Jack say somthing!"

Jack turned toward me then went down. I ripped his shirt to find the holes. I knew the bullets would have struck me except for him.

We were like twins after that. If he could live, the world was worth having. My feelings lived on my skin. We didn't have to speak, and he couldn't anyway. I didn't like the nurses buzzing around, I knew they wanted him. His bed was soaked with yellow ooze but I didn't leave. We moved to a second floor flat two months later. He was bandaged up but still knew how to put a sweet potato in slow.

I remember waking underneath Jack that first time. After I got loose, he said I was the only woman strong enough to roll him over.

"You just leave them pinned and suffocated."

"Nobody got hurt, but I guess it's possible."

"Not with me, it ain't."

He raised up to study my willfulness. He didn't mock it but his mood shifted. My silence formed questions only I heard though the word "love" lingered in my mouth like candy. I searched his body for dimples, admired his scars and brushed his hair. He loved me for not asking him to walk slower when we hit the avenues. Deep brown skin beaming into bronze. An unlined face, smooth as a table.

I asked what he wanted from his life and every answer had me in it. I feared for all the times I'd said "love' when he was shot. It was different when he was able to ask what "love" meant.

"Obstacles won't exist if you stick with me," Jack said at the dinner table.

"Besides me, what do you want?" I said.

His arms stiffened, silverware rattled, the table shook. Our closeness surprised me. He could move objects anytime he wanted but life doesn't care about one man's strength. Then again, who was I to judge weakness? Didn't I rush home to him when there were so many places I could go?

"I want to change your mind about life," Jack said, because he didn't know mystery. He believed life was hard because he had done hard labor. I knew life was hard because hunger don't rest. Papa and Mama died too early and I'm a woman that don't smile when nothing's funny.

Jack's family invited me to supper so they could look me over up close. I tried not to remember my cabin in the Hollows when I visited their place in New York. They had potted palms in the living room and lacy this and that. Memories are dangerous because Mama never had a pretty room and resentment come over my soul. My devil mind said, "You don't owe his people nothing!" I forced myself to hold down a plate of food I wanted to throw. If my aim was good, I'd break the mirror at the same time, then the windows. In my mind, the table we sat around flew through the air and didn't come back. Jack's mother put down her scrapbook and asked about my family pictures. Her voice was light and kind. I pretended all was cool. I said our snapshots were lost in a fire, because we never had any. Anger clamped my teeth but I managed a smile while drinking gin fizz. Jack sensed my mood and stayed close after the second one. His mother didn't say anything but probably knew I'd finished plenty of bottles by myself.

My Mama didn't have much, but she taught me to hide my angry reasons. Who would understand or care except them that suffer it? Thank goodness the first shock of alcohol slapped the shit out of my funk and erased the sadness of five minutes ago. Jack nudged my leg and smiled to ease my mood. A comfort flowed between us. I wanted him.

"I got a ring you might like," Jack said.

"What kinda ring?"

"What you think, Bessie?"

"Let's wait. Keep it like it is so love don't run and hide," I said.

"I'm crazy about you. Everything I ever wanted is you."

My mind ran for an exit. Memories of Earl Love caused my fingers to drum sad melodies. I never expected to hear words like this again.

"Bessie, you in a bad dream or what?"

"We got everything as it is, Jack. Getting married will ruin it. I'm telling you what I already lived. Let's call this being together."

"I'll show you 'together.' My nuts so tight I can hardly breathe. Can't sleep afraid you might leave. I prayed a ring might prove something."

I melted, wrapped like gifts under a tree. We married. I thought maybe trouble was over.

* * *

Clarence Williams was always ready with two or three songs he thought I was "born to sing." Don't get me wrong, Clarence was one of the first black songwriters that knew the blues was going to be big business. Dressed New York tight, Blake and Lyles style, with money to play, he didn't care who didn't want to see his black ass one more time.

"Look here, I'm the best. Nobody knows how to song plug and showcase colored talent better than me. Listen, Bessie, doors open because I deliver. I hear you making sad blue magic and lots of green bills with my tunes. My own mother broke down when I told her about you. I am not a pretend Negro. Ha-ha. You're already more famous than you know. The white won't let us get but so big. They pay us to sing for them then steal the interpretation. I know you been around. Word is you're next but won't happen without somebody on the inside. I'm the long shot coming fast on the rail, I'm a hound that can't be fooled. Walker over at Columbia wants a record, Bessie. He's looking everywhere for you," Williams said. His rabbit nose bobbed with each word.

"He wasn't ready five years ago," I said.

"He didn't forget those shows in Atlanta. He told me to, "find Bessie quick. Time is right.""

"What do you want out of this?"

"This is between friends, Bessie."

He faked innocence about as good as a whore, but I wanted to believe him. Williams looked at Jack hoping for a change in mood. Williams knew if he could get my man on his side, I'd be no problem.

"The white boys are thinking big. They discovered that our people want to hear themselves on the recordings. You heard of Sears Roebuck? They're ready to let black folk buy record players, stoves, you name it, on time. Just pay it off month to month. If you fall behind, they'll take it back. They're going to do phonographs like this and you know our people are going to have their music."

"That's nice, Clarence, but we got to go," I said.

"What I'm saying is important. Don't you see? The colored will be featured on records all over the world. This is different. Whole lot of money can be made if we're sharp." Clarence's words rushed past, one thought bumping the next like a schoolboy.

* * *

We moved in with Jack's family in New York to get ready for the audition with Mr. Walker. Jack's folks were cool with rehearsals at their place. Ruby, Jack's stage-struck niece, fell in with me one hundred percent. Her eyes spelled admiration from the first chorus. Her food got cold on account of watching me. That evening was when she first said "I want to know all about you," and that was no jive. She had a voice and nice legs so I showed her steps on the QT. Her people accused me of pulling her into show business but I can't make a grown person want to sing for their supper. She's crazy enough to want it or she's not.

Ruby heard "Bessie" this and "Bessie" that from Uncle Jack and was jealous of me at first. She said my warmth surprised her. I "glowed like a flame" when I entered a room. Everybody stopped to watch for a minute. She didn't know what to think. Ruby's family taught her to be ordinary, but after knowing me, Ruby wanted to stand out.

Jack made a big production of putting Mamie Smith's recording of *Crazy Blues* on the Victrola, a record the whole family loved.

> *I can't sleep at night*
> *I can't eat a bite*
> *'Cause the man I love*
> *He don't treat me right...*

"Now listen to Bessie singing this. Mamie is nothing compared to who's sitting across the table."

I sang from my chair and made windows rattle. Ruby's little mouth fell open all through the tune. Her shyness tickled me. She would never know what I went through to be here.

"Were you born with this? Did your Mama sing?"

"I learned in church and Chattanooga street corners. Me and my brother Andrew made noise every chance we got."

After dinner, I finished a cup of joe with a slow pour from the flask.

"Ruby, what else you want to know?"

"I didn't say anything."

"You always this shy? You look like a singer."

"Miss Bessie, that is the nicest thing anybody ever said about me."

"Sure 'nuff?"

She smiled like a child. Her dress shimmered like her lips.

"How did Uncle Jack meet up with someone so opposite of him?"

"Got a minute, dearie? It's real complicated," I said.

* * *

Clarence Williams, Jack and I took a cab to Columbia Records February 15, 1923. Williams made me nervous saying this recording session was "the biggest break of my life." Told me how to act and what not to say like I got this break by accident. He didn't do nothing for me at Okeh Records the month before, so I thought he shoulda let it rest. I was sick of him pretending to be family. Jack knew the record shop owner who tipped Williams about Walker looking for me. We were on to it from the first. Jack crossed and uncrossed his legs to make me laugh every time Williams lied. It was crowded in the back seat and every time Jack moved his big knees, Williams got bumped.

Mr. Walker couldn't have been nicer. He held my hand, introduced me to everybody but there was a dead feeling in the room. I felt like a bug under glass. Walker said I looked pretty so I showed off my diamond ring from Jack. I knew the stones weren't real but the other ofays acted like they knew something I didn't. They put me in front of a horn that was wired back to a control room. Williams played piano behind a sheet.

Walker cued me, "*T'aint Nobody's Bizness*, take one."

I sang all right but popped my "t"s and "p"s. Next time, I got ahead of the piano. Then, I fell behind, scrambled the lyrics. Williams dropped a cigarette in his own lap.

"Take seven."

I wanted a beer but Jack said no.

"Take eight."

"Take nine."

Back then the musicians couldn't hear what was recorded until the session was mastered. Walker decided if the performance was good enough to keep. I asked what he thought.

"Relax. One take was fine but the machine didn't record it."

Jack stayed nervous so I didn't look at him. I sweated through the new dress he bought for me. I told Williams he better lean on the keys more. He told me to stay out of drafts.

"Call it a day," Walker said.

"What you think, Williams?" I asked on the elevator.

"Damn tough. You're back tomorrow and you know the songs. He wants you or he'd have cut us off hours ago. You'll make it because there's nothing like you. Besides that, race records is hot. I saw it coming and know where it's bound. Since Mamie Smith broke out, the big money is ready to give the colored a chance. Don't worry about tomorrow. Walker knows you're 'it.' Just do what he says."

Williams spoke like a jackhammer, but he did take me to Walker and I owed him for that. Jack and I walked the boulevard, wondering what else could fail. His bigness was comfort, the rough sleeves of his coat a shield against the city.

Jack had to pee so Williams and I guarded the alleyway entrance. Voices floated above the sound of pissing. Jack heard my name, saw the engineer and Walker on the backstairs of the record company. He slid into a shadow and listened.

"The Smith girl sounded awful," the engineer said.

"What do you expect from a empty room and a bunch of white boys telling her what to do. No liquor, nobody talking back when she sings," Walker said.

"Excuse me for not being a nigger," the engineer said.

"You don't want to do this, do you?" Walker said.

"I'll record anybody but I don't have to like it."

"I say she's good. It's money in the bank if she can settle down for the microphone."

Jack tiptoed out and told what he'd heard. I didn't care what the cracker engineer thought long as Walker was behind me. Told Jack he was my good luck charm, huddled to him, matched his strides. If trousers had three legs, I'd have put one of mine in. Williams said New York was no town for amateurs, lucky we knew an honest brother like him. Jack cleared his throat but overplayed it and Williams realized he was being mocked.

"Don't believe what backbiters say. Negroes have to stick together. Think what I do is easy, Jack? I'm black and hungry as you and Bessie but the colored don't know how to stick together. No, we mistreat and back bite instead of trusting."

We listened but didn't say anything. Williams checked out the silence, tightened his tie, adjusted his pants so that the spats showed clean above his kicks, then stepped off the curb.

"Taxi! You and Bessie going my way? Okay, suit yourself."

Jack cupped my mouth with his palm.

"Let him go. Had enough of him today."

"He's got a point, Jack. He knows business."

"Not like I'm going to know it."

Jack's words felt like bricks and iron. I could build on them.

Next day, I wore a costume from my show in Atlantic City. It was flashy but kind of normal. I told Walker, I didn't like singing for a machine. My kind of music isn't lonely, it's made for a room full. He gave me an "Amen."

"Don't let worry close you down. Imagine you're at the 81 and it's half-past late. This ugly horn can make you famous."

Walker pulled a glass out of a drawer and poured me a drink. I knew I could win after that. The recording room door flew open after the second take.

"Give me a back up, just like that one. Blue as you can be!"

Williams was still pitching tunes when we left the studio without saying "bye." I could hardly speak or make sense of knowing I'd be famous from now on. A glow blossomed around Jack and me from inside out. We said nothing, shoulder to shoulder, leaning and stepping at the exact same time. Our eyes met and didn't disconnect because everything was possible. Jack's golden smile so bright against his lips. Every step said we couldn't wait to be alone together.

Chapter 15

*D*ownhearted Blues and *Gulf Coast Blues* came out real quick, sold 750,000 copies six months! I signed for fifteen hundred dollars worth of record sessions, exclusive contract with Columbia and hardly rested the entire year. Walker, Williams, Jack and me grinned, ginned, and planned into the evening.

"Bessie, do you know what you have done? You have made Columbia Records rich. Nobody colored ever sold near a million copies," Clarence Williams said.

"I ain't sold nothin' yet," I reasoned.

"No, no, no, Bessie. Think ahead, girl. You don't know what you got." He pleaded to manage me but Jack refused. Williams' next plea was to be my booking agent but Jack blocked him every time.

"What's the deal, Bessie? Has anybody else done more for you? Jack, what about those plans we made after the first session? Don't tell me you forgot that quick," Williams said.

"We talked but there was no promises."

"Those talks is how money gets made, brother. I'm not saying you promised me. I'm out for something but so is everyone else. You hold that against me? You think the record company not hustling? I believe in Bessie and you and what could happen for all of us. With her voice, my songs, we could..."

"But we ain't," Jack said.

"The white boy gonna close you out of the money, Jack. Negroes by themselves gonna miss this train."

I felt sorry for Clarence Williams but loved Jack's bulldog pride as my bodyguard, valet, and valentine. When he stood up, other men stepped back.

"I brought Frank Walker to you and now you think he's your color," Clarence said.

Jack flexed his arms, escorted me to the door. Williams sat tall as he could and popped his knuckles.

"I'm used to 'no' just like you, Bessie, and I'm not discouraged. You could do a whole lot worse than me."

We were in the hallway before Williams' pitch was through.

"OK, walk away. No hard feelings. I got more songs, Bessie. This isn't the last of me."

Golden doors had opened. Jack and I stepped into another world. Jack waited two days to buy my record and by then the stores had sold out!

"How'd you get popular so fast?" he said, wonder all in his eyes.

My time had come. He had forgot I'd been singing since childhood. He didn't know the back roads that led to this. It only mattered that Jack was proud like we had a baby. The summer light was soft and clear like a "down South" day had been shipped to New York just for us. I strolled the sidewalk like it was a stage apron, my heart swelled big as a tree. Hundreds of dollars in my purse and every store a temptation. My life had been spent "making do" but now wishing was same as having.

"Jack, baby, you want to walk to Harlem or would you rather get a cab? You want a cocktail or a whiskey still?" We laughed so hard we leaned on buildings to keep from falling. Jack saw a new Ford go by. "You want it?" I said with tears down his face and mine.

Wish I bottled the first year of fame to revive me when the thrill turned cold. All life's disappointment disappeared. No more waiting. Everything I'd prayed for was a sales slip away. Columbia put me on the road for weeks. I was mobbed everywhere but wasn't ready for the love I got. People took my hand and wouldn't let go. The applause when the curtains parted washed me with tears. Crowds shouted "Bessie!" and "Hometown girl!" Cheers and shouts about crushed the horns. Felt like I had angel wings. It was hard to keep lyrics straight. Applause like thunder claps. The beat and word got married, holidays only musicians celebrate.

I was allowed in the public's heart. Because I looked and sounded like them, they thought they knew me.

"Sing it girl." "Tell me these blues ain't bad." "I knew you in Atlanta" "Don't you remember my brother sister auntie knew your people in Louisiana. You from Tennessee? Well, must have been there then."

A black tide left the South and was on stage from Chicago to Baton Rouge. My verses cool as healing water. Every new record was like a letter from home. 1924, the first summer after fame, I thought about moving back to Chattanooga. Already got a big house for Viola and Tinnie and their kids, but this new house would be mine and Jack's. I wanted white porches, a big car with my name on it parked out front. Then I remembered I hated to keep house.

That's why a railroad car is my mansion and other people clean. I like to sit and watch the scenery for a minute, the moon and stars belong to me alone. I make them appear and vanish with a wave of my hand.

Jack and I returned to our flat in Philly and played house with big couches, satin sheets, custom suits for Jack, and lingerie for me. Had a kitchen full of chickens, gin, pig feet and beer plus the big Victrola, two telephones, telegrams, receipts, and shopping bags full of bills. "All this and sing too?" was how I felt about it.

"You concentrate on singing, I'll take care of the business."
Jack sucked a cigar and thought he knew how to handle cool green but I already had my brother Clarence and his wife Maud on the business end.

"Think it will come that easy?" I said to Jack.

"All Clarence Williams did was hustle and Walker's white."

"What's that supposed to mean?"

"Walker and his buddies run the records and Williams run to pick up the crumbs."

"You got a better plan?"

"My plan is to make us, you and me, the biggest thing in show business," Jack said.

"If you're going to put me in movies I want to vamp like Theda Bara."

"Ok, but you got to sing."

"You're right, you're right. Joke's on me. Movies got to talk before I can use them. When it does happen, who's going to be my Valentino?"

"I'm still learning, baby. Give it time."

"But you will get a plan."

"That's right."

"Like saying you were a detective when you were a security guard?"

"All I was trying to do was impress you."

"I guess I'll forgive it."

"Is your point I'm a liar who doesn't know to do anything?" Jack said.

"I guess I argued to find out who can get the best of the other."

"So playing a game?"

"Give me some sugar, Jack. You going on the road with me?"

"I'm going to prove what I'm talking about," he said.

"Make me happy if you do but if you don't, you're still number one."

"Listen here, Bessie. I came up New York fast while you were walking slow in Tennessee. I'm used to being free. Fast talking music types don't rattle me in the slightest. They are just part of the scenery."

"Don't preach, Jack. I put Clarence and his music aside because you are first, last and always."

"All I meant was that you came up hard and deserve all the success. Admit you were nervous in Atlantic City. People took a minute to get your style. Am I right or wrong? I sat up front because you knocked me out from the first. Fame has come like a wish come true. Nobody could have predicted it. Walker and the Columbia big shots said they saw it coming but they were shocked bad as anybody."

Jack did come to Atlanta after I wired about the crowds. He agreed there were too many bodies to count in the five block line. My music was hotter than a skillet. He shook his head at the pandemonium. I told him to throw his badge away, he could guard me full time. I was posed, interviewed, and put on the radio. They say mostly white people heard the broadcast but plenty of Negroes heard about my voice flying through the night. That's how blues and Bessie started to be the same thing. Once the colored heard the downbeat, they came running with the ofays right behind. Joe Oliver and the Hot Five, Jelly Roll Morton, St. Louis Blues. I was carried in the midst of it because blues explained life without cracking a book.

I bought new cars and sported furs into back alleys cross the tracks from Valdosta, Georgia to Chicago and nobody grudged it. I spent big money in dives because that's the company I keep. If the rich can't help nobody, who the fuck can?

Ruby, Jack's niece, worried me to death about wanting to sing and dance. It was alright with me but Jack put the squeeze on it last year.

"Ruby's a good girl. She doesn't understand what traveling is like," he said.

"She can be my company. She's pretty and can sing. What else does anyone need?" I said.

"Fine. She can be part of the act and take some of the pressure off me to travel. Deal?"

"Deal," I said.

I gave Ruby the courage to be alive. Taught her to stand for herself no matter what. If it came to blows, beat it back or fall. Ruby hadn't tasted freedom until I became her "Auntie."

"Where's your abandon, Ruby?"

"I didn't lose anything, Bessie."

"I mean abandon what people think, Ruby. Think they going to die for you?"

"No."

"Then why you living for what they think? Get in the damn car and have some of this brew."

I understood Jack way better than he knew. Coming up "down home" don't mean stupid but to him it did. I knew the difference between blood family and the outside world. Jack didn't understand about being black in the South. We signified "brother" and "sister" because how were we to know people passing by weren't "blood?" What the hell he think slavery meant? Up north too many lock their door and their manners. I ain't like that.

Jack's reading was hit-and-miss but he could be shrewd. I showed him the agreements between me and Columbia. He asked about some words, then kept studying while I cooked.

"That bastard," he said.

"Who?"

"Just do what I say tomorrow," was all he said.

Jack jerked open the door to Clarence Williams' office, striking his palm with his fighting fist. Williams went under the desk without a word but Jack dragged him out.

"How nice to see you, Bessie," Williams said while trembling a crooked smile.

"Bessie signed paper with Columbia Records. Nobody agreed to give you half her recording fee," Jack said.

That did it. I jumped Williams while Jack held him down. Tore up his music, knocked his glasses off. Jack baby tapped him a couple of times while I made a fist under the man's nose.

"Tear up Bessie's contract. It's your nuts if you don't."

Jack rifled the file cabinets like the cop he claimed to be. Williams pleaded, almost cried.

"Take my name off it. Tell Columbia I'll never belong to you,"
I said.

Williams scribbled so fast the paper tore. Jack pushed over bookcases
on the way out.

Next stop was my friend, Frank Walker. He didn't have anything to
do with Williams' back stabbing and gladly signed me to an exclusive
with Columbia. We walked out with $350, as near happiness as we'd ever
be. Walker had me recording again in less than two months. There was
no nervousness this time, the recording horn was mine to play. My throat
discovered half tones and growls that echoed the brass. Didn't need a
drummer to keep the beat. I wasn't paying somebody to drown me out.
The first sessions were hard because the room felt cold, wasn't anything
like the life I came from. I learned how to choose notes in the clubs where
people cursed you out if the music didn't move them. I wrapped a sound
around what I lived and didn't leave the funky butt out. Not every note is
worth singing. I choose tones that lay up in your heart.

Success paid the bills but so much time got eaten by details. No more
small gigs. The white variety acts didn't outspend me. We had first class
sets, costumes, a cast of thirty including musicians, dancers, support acts
and roustabouts. I prided myself on the best show anywhere. Nobody
slacked off long as I headed the bill.

To keep the peace, I let Jack think counting money was the same
as being the manager. He was proud to say "Bessie Smith Productions"
on the phone. One day Jack saw some accountants with their yellow
bookkeeping pads. Next day he had Maude order that same kind of
paper. The piano player told him the income tax required receipts so
Jack pretended he had saved them. Later on, Jack went to another office
and noticed the clerks had light green ledgers. He threw out the yellow
pads and we only wrote on seafoam green ones from then on. He believed
if things looked right, the situation was handled. Loved those straight
gray lines mixed with the red ones. His bank deposits neat as bricks in a
wall, numbers straight and clean as a schoolboy's.

"Why did you sign on for another week in Chicago, Bessie?"

107

"Because the show's so sold out. No use throwing money away."

"I promised my Mom you'd be at her birthday next week."

"Walker said Columbia can't keep up with requests for my appearances."

"She was expecting you."

"I know she'll understand. We'll get her something nice."

"Mother was counting on seeing us together, Bessie."

"Walker says 'Success is a sacrifice.'"

"I wanted a shorter tour and higher salary for you but you're so rich, a raise doesn't matter. Every time Walker says 'jump' you're flying over the moon singing a song."

"Shut up, Jack."

"You know it's true."

"You're the one who wanted to be on tour," I said.

"I hardly see you. You're on the phone or out on 'business."

"And you're taking care of a lot of things."

"Not really, I feel like I'm in the way. Clarence and Maud are who you depend on. I'm only the husband. You coming to the hotel or going out?"

"I need a drink, Jack."

"You have liquor at the hotel."

"It taste different in a bar. Come and ball with me, Jack."

"I'm going to Philly tomorrow morning. Got some fishing to do after the birthday party. Another thing. I need a hundred this time. You cool?"

"Alright, Jack. Get Mother Gee some flowers. OK?"

"Tell Maude about the hundred because I don't want a fuss," Jack said.

"There'll be no fuss and I'll be home 'fore you know it."

"Tonight?"

"Please, Jack."

"That word 'please' has a meaning, Bessie."

"Don't start."

"There's talk..."

"About?"

"You."

"And you believe the stage door shit?"

"I don't believe all I hear. But I wonder," Jack said on his way out. "Call me, Bessie, I probably won't see you again until the tour ends."

"What about later this morning?" I said.

"There's a milk train tonight connecting to Birmingham and I'm on it."

"Why you like this, Jack?"

"No, why are you like you are is the question."

"I still love you baby," we both said at the same time.

The way I see it, where I go after work is my business. I'm married but no one should predict what I might do. I liked to think there were no witnesses to my pleasures; that I kept play and marriage separate. I didn't seek other men for a long while but women's pretty fingers made me high. Sometime a business call, innocent as can be, got personal. My "company" knew my situation, yet ran to me for shade on a sultry day. Crushed my sincere will with nipples and kisses while I tried to be good.

After a big show in Chattanooga, people sprouted from rusty logs. Viola and Tinnie sat down front, beside themselves with all that had happened for me. Fuck a twenty or a fifty, I pressed C-notes in my sisters' hands and kissed them hard. Jack had returned to Philly and I was feeling fine. Friends, strangers, including those who mocked me when I was black-ass poor, had to shake my hand. I didn't change because my name was plastered on a wall. The good old dives were still good, the down home food was my meat. I'd wandered alone somewhere close to where I thought Mama, Papa and Bud was buried. Nobody knows how I hoped to hear them say, "Well done, Bessie, well done."

The audience wouldn't let the show end, but I walked after five encores. Afterwards, some pals and I took our long skirts to a muddy alley looking for a fish fry.

"Bessie, how does it feel to be back?" a new pair of sweet eyes said.

"Like I ain't never left."

"If I got out of here, these streets wouldn't see me once."

"Well, I'm leaving soon," I said.

Her laughter was full but not loud. I congratulated myself on being good for over a year then moved to her side of the table. I left to get drinks but came back to an argument between this girl and an old man. I looked away the very instant the bastard pushed this beauty down. I reached for her, got sucker punched, but came back and broke a chair on him.

"Bessie you shouldn't have done that. He'll get you," sweet eyes said.

Her fear and gratitude made my love come down. I took the girl to a private room. All I did was praise, make plans and wonder at my luck. In the wee hours, I was saying goodbye, paying the bill, when the son of a bitch I took off Sweet Eyes sneaked back and stabbed me. The room disappeared but her eyes never left mine.

"Can you hear me, Bessie?"

She didn't care about the blood on her dress and arms, all she cared about was me. She cradled me into the cab, even said the whole thing was her fault. I wanted her like a thirst but we never met again.

Ruby and Maud was bedside when I woke up next day. No profit in

110

being hospitalized. Patched and swollen, the Empress limped to the train. SRO for weeks ahead, booked and bound to go.

Fletcher Henderson, composer and arranger for some of my best sides, wouldn't stop talking about "Armstrong, Armstrong." He finally got the trumpet wiz on calendar. Of course I'd heard about Dipper and King Oliver and the Chicago cats but we'd never met. There he was at my session in 1925, scrubbed and cute as a button. We wailed *St. Louis Blues* and *You're A Good Old Wagon But You Done Broke Down* like kids in a playroom. We were born for that day. Those records will never die.

Chapter 16

Mugsie, one of my ex-showgirls, held the boy's hand like she wasn't sure she could let go. Years before, I promised to make a home for "Snooks" if she ever needed my help. Her eyes filled with water. She had too many children and not enough husbands. She knew I was crazy about the boy. I told her to not worry about being forgotten. Blood is blood. Good intention poured out of me. The boy lived for my visits and since I came South several times a year, he'd still be part of his mother's life. I wasn't quite on the earth.

"You're keeping your railroad car? I never even dreamed about having anything that beautiful," Mugsie said.

"You rode in it for a whole tour," I said.

"Yes I did, and it was like a fairy tale."

"Snook's gonna have what the white boys have," I said.

"I'm happy for him, I'm happy for you because you love him, but..."

"Can't give him up Mugsie? I don't blame you. Take your time."

Her lip quivered and she couldn't look at me good. "It ain't fair to wait longer. I'm have to let him go. You love him. He love you too but he's still my child and I can't keep from crying."

I told her to look for Snooks later in the year. She could call my private number anytime. I'd save the railroad car for when he grew up and owned a train line. Or maybe he'd be a doctor or big lawyer. I wrote my address and phone numbers twice and left it in the envelope I'd promised. I wasn't buying her child; he'd always be hers. She wobbled her head on my breast and I let her hold the boy long as she wanted.

"I'm happy for Snooks because you got the world in a jug."
She kissed her child good bye in my big car. She rubbed his head then held my chin in her hand. We drove away and didn't stop until I spied a phone booth in Macon.

"Jack, it's Bessie. Say hello to your new son."

The boy laughed and then gave me the phone before racing back to the car.

"Are you happy, baby?" I said, wanting a feeling from Jack more than words. I autographed an envelope someone handed me. I remember saying, "This is my boy. This is my heart."

"How about we call him Jack, Jr. so he'll be more family?" Jack said.

A crowd gathered around the car.

"If we do right, the boy will bring us together."

"We'll be like everybody else now," Jack said.

"Baby makes three," I said.

Someone yelled my name and waved. I turned my back to the street.

"Promise we can do it," I whispered, more to myself than to him.

"What did you say? It's a bad connection."

I blew a kiss then ran with my child to the car.

Back in Philadelphia the boy's fortune was read and all the signs were good. Jack's fingers covered mine and the boy's like a giant leaf. One of the dancers said the boy looked like us and we pretended he did. Now that we had Jack Jr., I rented a house for Viola, Laura and her baby, and the house beside it for Tinnie & Lulu and her children. They had begged to leave Chattanooga so why not bring them to Philly? Viola tried to raise me so I knew she could handle Jack Jr. when I was on the road. Jack and I were back in love's hands and there was no reason to remember tears.

Chapter 17

"Just how rich are you, Bessie?" Tinnie said after seeing her new house.

"Richer than you can count to," I said.

"There's got to be a number," Tinnie said.

"Bessie doesn't have as much as she thinks," Jack said. I pushed his ribs but he looked at my sister and didn't blink.

"You'll always have enough," I said in hopes he'd stop worrying me.

"Viola, you been dragged through hell since Mama and Papa passed. It all came on you but now it's your time again. You got a home and a new start, the family together again."

"I just want to thank you Bessie. I never..."

"That's alright. I told you life was gonna smell different one day."

"Do you see how things got to be different?" Jack said when we were alone. My right eye opened wide as an owl's.

"We got a family of our own now," he said.

"I see that, Jack."

"You think Viola and the rest see it?"

"Of course. They're family, too."

"How many families we going to have?" At least he came out with it quick.

"We got my sisters and a brother. One helps the other."

"Is it your husband's turn yet?" I was wide-awake and worried.

"I see you helping them more than your husband."

"You forgetting they're family?"

"Don't raise your voice Bessie. We're just talking, now. Are they more family than I am?"

"You're my husband."

"I'm more like a step-child. Thought time would change things."

"I'm rich, Jack. What would I look like forgetting my people?"

"A drought can come," he said.

"If I got a roof how you think I can forget about them?"

"Why can't they understand you and me aren't their parents? They are in-laws."

"They're my sisters. They're my blood."

"Don't be getting hot, Bessie. They got their own house, groceries, clothes, because you're Santa Claus. They're gonna spend us into the poor house."

"Us? Now it's 'us', is it? I made the damn money. Open my mouth and the dollars come for all of us. I promised them before I met you that they wouldn't want for nothing."

"See how it's changed, Bessie. Back when we were fresh to each other, it wasn't about yours and mine. It was 'us.' What about the boy? Where do you and me start and your sisters end?"

"Don't tell me to put my family out."

"Be reasonable, Bessie."

"You be reasonable. You don't say nothing when your car note is paid, the clothes, the liquor. What do you have to complain about?"

"I'm your husband, Bessie. You complain if I don't take the money. You complain if I do. I stand by you, I do what you say do. Now tell me I'm a lie."

"I'm tired of talking. What is the use of being rich if it only brings trouble? This is why I need a drink."

"Where are you going, Bessie?"

"Kiss my ass."

116

"What will I do when the boy gets home from school?"

"You his daddy. Take him to a ball game."

Jack knew I'd get home after the gig and not be able to sleep. I wanted to please him, but I'm a night owl when I'm working. I invited him to party until it got futile. Jack was good for one maybe two clubs a night and agreed that it made sense to put him in a cab once he'd met his limit. We were still tight but shows that gave him goose bumps got harder to find after the first year. Playing cards on a train was not his thing. He never understood what a thrill it was to guarantee a full house night after night in a different town. The buildup to fame isn't the sweetest. The long run has the real sugar, the proof that success is no joke. The more Jack pulled back, the more I got my way. Bessie blossoms when the hour is late. If I don't let her out, the pretty bird won't sing. Tried to school Jack about who he married. I dusted him with magic bubbles, made him pretty as a movie star. If we'd been white, who knows what might have been.

After he got a little wise, he'd curse out the girl on my lap though it wasn't nothing, yet.

"Guess you want to forget I'm your husband."

"I ain't forgot nothing, Jack. I know who you are."

"Then why you treat me so bad? I don't like these women pulling at what's mine."

"You think that's what we're doing? Pulling on ourself? Doing what boys do."

"Why you have to be so obvious, Bessie?" he said, afraid someone might hear. He liked sex but talking about it made him shy.

"You started it."

"Guess I made a mistake."

"I needed to stay and you had to get home."

"I want you, Bessie."

"Somebody call a cab?" The cab driver parted the crowd looking for Jack.

"All you gals ain't got a man, go see Bessie. She likes funny business."

He was drunk, looking for a fight. My boon coon buddies tried to hide their smirks behind sleeves and turned heads. They can kiss my ass. I saw Jack's face when he left out. Our love was slipping down. It should have been clear long before I wasn't the proper little lady. How many women that description front a band and sell thousands of records singing blues? I thought about the ground that held my mother, father, and brother, the babies that didn't live but a day or two. Thought of the markers I'd buy if I knew where to stick them.

After I became Empress of the Blues, there didn't seem to be any problem money couldn't handle. I rocked stages so tough audiences forgot they had to breathe. That tinny sound called Bessie on the Victrola was just a teaser for seeing me live. *Reckless Blues, Gulf Coast Blues, Put Me in the 'Lectric Chair,* are powerful because it's just me, the microphone and a squeaky bed.

Ruby and I got to Birmingham a day early and intended to rest but Ma Rainey was in town, so I took her to meet the Songbird. The Georgia Jazz Band droned into the floor and I couldn't stay still. The beat cooled my mind, notes simmered and popped from a trumpet full of heat.

The stage was dark, a dirty curtain jerked back. A cardboard Victrola was stage center, three blue spots, every shadow purple black. A cymbal ticked. The Victrola opened. Ma Rainey stepped out into a key spot. People sprang from their seats hollering "Phantom" like she was Lon Chaney. The crowd surged the stage. Nothing the ushers could do but hope there wasn't a fire. Fat and short made no difference. When she pulled her shoulder back, a drum exploded. There weren't any dead spots, every song hot as a candle.

The three of us found a corner backstage during intermission. She thanked me for bailing her out of jail in Chicago, but she knew wild women save their own.

"Them police was serious though. When they raided the party and found a bunch of sisters without a man, them cops figured it was pussy time. They bragged about whores giving them some," she said.

"They come out and ask for it?"

"Girl, what you think? One of them cops was already showing his in the wagon. I told him we all had the clap. Fool said he didn't care. I said I could make bail and a little extra when they produce a phone."

"That's where I come in."

"That's right. Empress of the damn blues. Ain't that something?"

"Then you're the Queen, Ma."

"No, baby. I'm just Ma, can't wear no crown. You carry it off like you never had to worry where your next bowl of greens is. You got it all."

I got shy. Her congratulations meant something, her arm about my neck, her fingers lightly tapping.

"How's your husband? Doing you right or hardly doing?"

"My luck hadn't run out. I like playing the homebody when the tours are over. I have to find calm sometimes."

"What you do for fun?" she said, her hand on my chin, her face a breath away. Gold charms hung from a sash around her head. Platinum bracelet, her mouth full of new gold. Pearl earrings. Diamond watch. If things went wrong, everything but the teeth could be sold.

I ignored Ruby while she watched my every move. Ma covered my hand, said she didn't know what a regular day would resemble. If I was halfway happy, then she was too.

"I'm tired of running after Cinderellas. I take 'em to my castle but they end up missing the prince."

"You going back to Pa?" I asked with a smile. She scratched her neck.

"Don't know where he is. Wished I'd had a child. Gives you a reason to live stable."

"Getting tired of the road, Ma?"

"I keep myself amused. Always a young boy nice to look at. Some of them even want me for awhile."

Pratfalls and squeals drifted backstage. Drum drops, sharp as knives, rose to the catwalks. Ma worked her gums with a toothpick. She told Ruby to find us some Coca Colas.

"Why don't you marry one of those boys?" I said.

"About the time I get them trained, they practice on somebody else," she said.

"You don't want them anyway, Ma."

"I ain't going to have anybody, Bessie. That's why I save my money. Buy yourself a record company before they learn you got a brain."

I didn't answer because I was strong and young. I had bookings straight into next year but didn't want to brag. Stage lights went from yellow to reds. The floor vibrated.

"How long you going to stay married, Bessie?"

I answered slowly.

"Depends on Jack."

"You're comfortable?"

"I come back to him and he comes back to me," I said.

"To you or for you?"

"I can't tell the difference."

"What about the boy? "

I bragged about his good looks and sweet disposition. She rubbed her palms, held my face between them.

"Don't forget to divorce Jack when it's over. Don't leave him anything he doesn't deserve." She rested her palms on her knees.

"You know I'm not that stupid," I said.

"It's not about that. Put a rope on your dreams. Lead' em to the barn."

Ma flashed her crowded smile. Too many teeth in one mouth. You don't envy her until she sings.

"You're down on men, period," I said.

"I ain't giving an old man my money. I can't argue about who's the boss. I wake up when I want to. The women know how to soothe me."

"You do wear those mannish suits," I said.

"And I sweep the shit and bury the dead ponies. You're in the big theaters, but I still play Cotton Clubs in the fields. You remember them sisters wearing gunnysack shifts and granny bonnets. You been there! They stand on chairs and their men can't set them down. They say 'Go on Ma, wear a tie. You can't make no babies, but you free.' These moments bring tears to my eyes."

"I got everything but something is missing," I said without looking up.

Ma sat up then rocked left to right. Just watching her cooled me. She worried that her insides were damaged. I asked what the doctor said but she fluttered her hands and shimmied her chair to a secret tempo.

"My doctor ain't nothing but a quack."

Ma adjusted her beads, fluffed her hair.

"Everything we got came from poor-ass houses on a dirt street."

"That's who we are," I said.

"Wish I owned a theater to play in when nobody else wants me."

"You'll always have a crowd, Ma."

"I don't know about that. These movies are fixing to push out the singers," Ma said.

"I figure they help sell my show. I been loving the flickers since Chattanooga days."

"Be careful, Bessie. If these movies start talking, we're in trouble. I heard a record man say blues is playing out."

"Says who? I can't keep enough seats for the crowds. Besides, we make our living off our voice. The talkies might be our way to Hollywood."

"You're red hot now ain't you? Save your money so you don't have to sing on the freak show."

"I'm still young, Ma."

"Not forever. No forgiveness for being an old woman," she said.

"But everything's going your way."

"Been on the road since 1900, Bessie. I was in the Blackberries. Married Pa in ought four. Minstreled, toured, carried the blues every place would have me. Now I need a fancy bus to keep up with your railroad car. You done priced me out."

"Heard about that, did you?" I said.

"Seen it too, but I want wheels on the ground. Don't care to wait for an engine to hook me up. When I got to go, I'm gone."

She had a point. Ruby returned with the drinks but gushed over Ma's career too much.

"Hush," I said.

It was near show time. I walked Ma to the edge of the curtain. The band vamped under blue gels to a full house. Ma pointed out the drummer.

"I dress and undress him like I want," she said.

I agreed he was fine but she knew I wasn't impressed.

"Thought you were a ladies' girl," I said.

"I need a change just like you do," she said.

The band kicked into double time. Ma invited me to sing but we just kissed goodbye. Ma didn't need me or nobody else to carry the show. I had so much to tell her but feared to do it.

It was true that movies were getting more and more popular. Most of my shows began after the pictures ended but I was still the headliner. Our visit had been sweet so why piss on it with problems? Still, I felt like a singer without a record. Will I ever match her? We're friends. These feelings not even worth thinking about yet I got to argue with myself. I feared the audience would wash Ma Rainey's toilet just to hear one more song. Knowing this left great emptiness around my fame.

Ruby asked too many questions in the cab.

"Didn't Ma look tired? Why didn't you sing when she asked you?"

Fact is Ma and me were working hard when she was sucking milk and she still kept talking. Having it soft coming up made her stupid. If she'd had a little bit of my life she'd have more sense. I hit the car seat and told the driver to get me home. Took a silk scarf off Ruby. That shut her up. She trembled like I might attack. Good thing I didn't have to go on stage because a nerve was loose and I didn't know how to fix it.

"If you got any questions, ask Ruby," I told the driver.

"What did I do? What did I do?" was all Ruby could say when I went off. That's when life got quiet as a snowfall. Lord knows she wasn't going to fight me. She wasn't like that. Never was never will be. Always stayed sweet against my storming. She admired me too much.

The cabbie checked his mirror afraid he'd picked up a dangerous fare. I thought seeing Ma would make me happy but I left feeling angry. Liquor made me shout "kiss my ass" to the buildings and people waiting to cross streets. Made them glare at me like I was the bogeyman. This happened when I ignored everything but my moody self. When the demons landed, I didn't care what anybody thought and wouldn't change to please you. Sometimes a boozy Bessie was a picnic but a drunk Bessie went to war. Ruby got caught between Jack and me more times than necessary. She even told me that Jack wanted her to tattle when I stepped out of line. I should have been grateful but got mad because she kept it to herself for awhile.

"Ruby, you don't know nothing about nothing. Liquor is the gate to pleasure. Ain't never had sex with a man cocaine stiff? You don't know fuck, but after tonight you won't need to be told twice."

Chapter 19

My old flame from Birmingham pumped liquor to the Southside through Al Capone. Richard Morgan's crib was a brownstone four floors high where kings of rhythm lounged with girls, cards, and brew. I'm talking about Armstrong, Ma Rainey, Ellington. They're streamlined, don't break in if your mind's slow.

The party was train station loud before Richard made the crowd "listen to a great artist." I bowed to the room while "Fatha" Hines churned the keys. He felt hot as a honeymoon, my tones velvet sweet. The crowd couldn't get enough and I didn't blame them. Thought they'd heard some blues before but my notes sent something new up the registers. I haunted the party with ambition. "Tell your girlfriend singing in the shower to forget it, Bessie's on the scene." The gamblers listened with folded cards, gangsters begged for thrills they'd never have. I had my dimples on. I told a drag queen who tried to sing with me, "You gotta have a real pussy to sing my song."

"What makes you think I don't?" she answered. I sang until Richard rescued me.

"I know you're married, but it's no crime to dream you're not," he said. I banked Richard's words and never forgot his kindness.

* * *

The gypsy warned me to open my palms and feed my heart. I gave her more money. She said beware of depending on fame and anger at things I couldn't see.

"What do you mean?" I said, but she shook her head and turned the cards face-down.

"You're a store house, Bessie. Feelings come to you like phone calls when you're singing. You answer every one and don't hang up," she said.

"What? Talk sense."

"Listen. It will never be easy and you won't know the meaning until the end. Somebody chose you. I can't say who. They..."

"They? You talking about God?"

"I can't name what was listening before you was made but they had to hear your song one more time."

"You're a crazy gypsy and that's a fact."

She invited me to her parlor. I pointed to the Victrola and said I paid for that. She put on *Backwater Blues* recorded when my voice was full and wide.

I wrote that record because my show got stranded by a storm and we had to be rowed through a flood. Kept on raining. Housetops were pyramids in the river. Hopes were down, bricks turned to sugar, wood to paste. My car floated toward Detroit. Cows and dogs corralled by downed trees. We climbed from the second story waving towels. I kissed the ugly boatman who said he couldn't let the blues drown. Upside down world, the ground useless and lost, the sound of water folding over paddles, water collapsing glass, houses turned into fishbowls. My showgirls wouldn't stop whimpering. We sailed in a bad dream, all of us leaves in the stream. I stopped looking down but decided I'd rather drown than burn. A thousand dollars in my underclothes but damned if I'd let the turtles find it. The boatman tried to kill a snake swimming by, like that could stop the rain. The sky locked just above our heads, pressed clouds flat as sheets. Hills looked like skulls in the water. Sheets tied to trees. Branches threw punches. Voices begged but there was no more room. All we could do was promise to tell somebody. I stood on a soaked levee that evening and hummed a prayer for the homeless people, the ones who disappeared like days.

❧ **Chapter 20** ❧

It was late afternoon, the sky ready to fade. The hotel room was smoke damaged, but it was a step up from a rooming house. It didn't matter what town it was and I didn't care about a view. My clothes and makeup were still on the bed. I was combing a wig when he slipped in.

"Surprised, Bessie?" Jack had practiced the line so that there was no welcome in it. He knew I wouldn't appreciate its rudeness.

"You know how to say hello?" I said.

All the days we lived without each other were stacked between us. His tight mouth and stiff arms said more than his words.

"Hello can wait. Where have you been?"

If I answered, he'd go ten steps further. Next thing I'd have a diary to mail home.

"Playing cards with Ruby. You don't have to be sneaking up on me."

"Who else was with you last night?"

Jack could snarl and yet smile. Leaves from the tree rattled beside the window.

"Why you want to start something, baby? I'm all for you."

"Think I'm blind, Bessie?"

Jack couldn't have known about my girl in Florida; that was a week ago. A young man and I had some moments but he was already involved with one my dancers. I hadn't been drunk more than twice in a month. I moved closer, ready to forgive, but Jack brushed my hand back. I looked up. Couldn't let him sucker punch me.

"You come all this way for trouble?" I said, warning him. My eyes said trust me, let me find a way. Ma Rainey always had a gun but I never thought I'd need one. He turned a chair backwards and sat down. His eyes were hidden in cigarette smoke. I sat on the bed and lit one of my own to slow the mood down. He was thick and direct. Wished I had a door between us.

"Couldn't call your husband one time while he's sick at home."

"I didn't know you were sick."

My voice dragged because I knew I'd thought so little about him. The road had erased Jack.

"I was puking with fever and your funny business is no secret. Think hearing how wild you are was helping me get well? What about that yellow boy in the tight pants at the card game?

Disgusted, he killed the cigarette, pushed me down on the bed. I wasn't afraid but I pleaded.

"That boy dances in my show. He doesn't have anything I want."

"Heard you bought him drawers to match yours."

"That's a damn lie," I said.

"When I take down that boy's pants they better be different." He tried to strip me. I doubled up and pushed him but he'd come to fight. The blows didn't stop until I broke the mirror with a perfume bottle. We both had glass in our hair and tiny cuts. Pieces of mirror showed the fucked up room. We leaned against separate walls.

"Look what you did, Bessie."

"Like beating me is OK but don't break the mirror?."

I ran out stinking like violets. Ruby was downstairs and heard everything. She ran right with me dodging cars, slipping through alleys. I was really scared this time. We hid in a rooming house across town until sundown. I played the night curtain peepin' and hidin'. Folded the show, gambled that Jack wouldn't follow me to the next city. We're no good for each other but we don't break off.

I called him between shows a week later and somebody else picked up the receiver. Jack didn't breathe like that.

128

I said, "Who's there?" several times.

"Nobody, baby. I'm lonely for you."

"I called to talk about you and me," I said.

"Your family is between us. Stumbling because their hands are chained to your purse, your food in their mouth."

"I should send all my money to you, I suppose."

"That sounds more right than sending your money to Viola. She ain't your man, is she?"

"She ain't knocked me down yet."

It was his turn to go quiet.

"Why would I bring harm when you been so good to me?" he said

"I thought that too but you've blacked my eyes and busted my lips," I said."

"You want to keep trading stories about who's worst? I stepped between you and a bullet. Deny it, Bessie."

"I've always been grateful for that. The question is what do you know about money? You can hardly read, Jack. Viola puts the checks in the bank. She can't get money I don't give her."

"And I couldn't do that" he said.

"You might not. You're too much like me. Mistakes happen. If you lost my money none of us could live."

"Have it your way, Bess. I'm looking for my own, now. I've turned selfish too."

He hung up before I could answer. Took the show back on the road, called Jack from Memphis a week later. I had a mink bag full of coins. Closed the door on a white woman who wanted me to give up the booth. I wanted to hear about the boy. Was he still happy? I forgot about this when Jack answered the phone saying "Bessie Smith Productions" like he promised. I got that old feeling because his voice was full of loneliness.

"Baby, the phone's always ringing. Baltimore, Atlanta, Florida. Ever been down there where the waves tumble sweet and soft?" he said, trying to make me weak.

I said Memphis was cold but the show got nothing but raves. Folks mob me and don't even try to pick my pocket. They tell me I'm as big in real life as I seem on stage and I take the compliment. Some think I sing their thoughts. One girl said her boyfriend beat her. I told her a hard dick is easy to find, while boyfriend held her hand but didn't say nothing.

"I found a better house for just us," Jack said. "$8,000 cash, five rooms. I told them you'd take it."

"I don't believe you, Jack. You couldn't get the money without Maud letting me know."

"Ok, you caught me."

"Why you lie so much?"

"Why you trick so much?"

"Forget it Jack. It's all gone to hell."

My money, his plans. He talked Maud into letting him schedule shows. Booked me into St Augustine and Miami the same night. I sweat while his feet are on a desk. We argued about him getting too familiar with my signature.

"Even gold mines tap out," I said.

Jack still could be sweet, though. He kept the celebrity telegrams and rave reviews in a special box so he could read a bunch at a time to me. He kept a crate of my records to sell in barbershops. His wrists were the size of most men's ankles. He had to come through a door sideways. His teeth like a picket fence in a hard head big as mine. Why couldn't he be smart too? The tour ended and I went home to Jack. Why was I was so optimistic? He'd hung up the phone at the sound of my voice at least twice while I was on the road. I wasn't sure I had a marriage when the key turned to an empty house. My unopened telegrams lay on a table and no use pretending I wasn't disappointed. I phoned his buddies to say, "I'm back and ain't waiting forever."

Before long, his heavy thumping feet broke my rest.

"Don't act surprised," I warned him and managed not to curse. It was a worn out evening, his suit coat over his arm. Perfect for a gun, but Jack wasn't a killer.

"You want me out? I got places lined up."

"I know this place is mine," I said, getting out of bed.

"What happened to us, Bessie?"

"You mean before I was your punching bag," I said.

"Like I'm the only one who's wrong?" he said.

Our voices rose. I wanted a set of rooms that didn't change, a hallway that didn't end in a stage, a bathroom that belonged to me. Jack's body seemed soft and caved in. Tough disappointment breathed between us and nobody dreamed storybook stuff. He held me until I gave in. I refused to speak, only listened to the shuffle of our feet. He couldn't dance but we two-stepped by the table lamp. I decided words caused the trouble. We stumbled into sex.

I remembered Chattanooga after the fire, the talk in the ashes, the house dying like a person. What would I remember about Jack if this place burned down tonight? I moved closer to him but thought about breaking a light bulb in my fist. I remembered Atlanta concerts with lines that went for blocks but couldn't recall my dead brother's voice or the taste of his fingers. Jack kissed me and I dared to kiss him back.

* * *

Cooking calmed my mind. In better days, the apartment smelled like greens and black-eyed peas when I was off the road. The box played jazz and I didn't listen to blues unless someone begged. I was tired of my own voice and hated how my songs were trapped and couldn't change. I wore my robe and house shoes days at a time because that meant freedom:

No place to go, no place I had to be. I'd have married myself if I could. Two days later, I hoped this fit would pass.

"Why don't you get dressed? I want to go to the show."

He lied. The man didn't want to walk in alone. I gave in, had some drinks, but my mind was capricious. I didn't pay attention to his conversation and he didn't care because he was in love with himself too. When Jack went silent in his tortoise shell head, it was a blessing to me.

Columbia sold fifty-three thousand records off just four sides in the summer. I was riding high. People stood by the tracks in powdery dust to see my yellow Pullman roll from Norfolk to Dallas. Black as I was, there was my name, bright green as money, on the best rail car money could buy. It could sleep forty, had its own galley and flush toilets, my pick of musicians and girls. It was no dream, everything the way I wanted it. Money changes everything.

Steel grinding steel, leaving Louisiana bound for Houston, the train slowed to take on water. I was almost asleep when the girls pounded my door shouting "Raise the curtain!" I heard a "Oh God have mercy!" There was this woman dangled off the tree. Her head paid no attention to the rest of her body. The dancers leaned on me like I knew what to do. Their faith was humbling. The tree was a few yards off the tracks. Gray poles and harsh light from a blood moon. We ran barefooted to a nightmare. I never expected to see this 'cause I don't dwell on bad luck. Got so rich I thought I wouldn't have to taste every tear.

> *Once I lived the life of a millionaire.*
> *Spending my money,*
> *I didn't care...*

This song warned me, the audience, anybody that things change in a moment. My breath raced ahead of thoughts. I had to slow the vomit down.

"We can't stay. Another train coming directly," the black brakeman shouted. The air felt electric, his plain words burned. The white folk stood by the front cars. One with a badge said, "She's dead" like "Hello, how are you?"

"Bring her in my car. I'll take her home."

"Miss Bessie, you can't put a dead woman on my train," the conductor said. The sheriff stood behind him.

"It's my damn car. I own it. Nobody telling me what to do with my car."

"The railroad don't belong to you or to me," the conductor said.

"I'm talking about my private car. You need permission to even visit my car. Now you telling me what I can't do?"

The railroad dick looked like he wanted to get into it so I gave him a chance.

"You know who killed her, Bessie?" he said.

"How could I know?"

"I guess you can put her in your car. I know the railroad don't want this by the tracks. Soon as we get to a siding, I'm leaving the body there and you and the sheriff can argue over it," the conductor said.

"You don't know nothing about her, Bessie," the others said.

"She black like us. Humans can't stand but so much. We ought to carry the girl like the sisters did Jesus from the cross," I pleaded like a church girl. My mouth couldn't keep up with my mind. "Why it always got to be us burned like leaves?" I paced and cursed so far from prayer.

"They lynched a man in Chattanooga when I was young. I wasn't supposed to go but I saw the colored men take him down from the bridge. I was just a child. Would have been home if Papa was alive."

Clarence and some other men stood between me and the dead girl. I tried to get past.

133

"We can't help her. You know it's true," Clarence said while Maud held my hand. We wrestled like kids. Bad hiccups came. I vomited a poison taste from another time. My guts ached. Who was this sister and why was she dangling on a limb like a mail bag?

"We can't get in this. We can't make it right," the men said. "It's a shame 'fore God but..."

Some of us heard a moan, wasn't just me.

Blues runs around my house,
in and out of my front door.
Can't eat, can't sleep, so weak
I can't walk my floor.

"The girl hasn't done nothing," the dancer said. He had stuff running out of his nose. "Oh I seen it before," he cried. "She's dead because she was by herself. That's how the crackers do."

The wind's dirty blade scraped my lips. The brakeman said the engineer was gonna leave. The steam warned us. I shook like wet fingers in a light socket.

"Get on the train, Bessie," Clarence said.

I wouldn't move until Maud led me back to my Pullman. I knew we had to go. The train jerked like it might stall but finally rolled. It would have been better if the train left me there. Mama and Papa would have said the dead girl was family. And I left her! The stateroom was funky with sweat and anger. I poured liquor and remembered why revenge felt like justice. It rained alcohol. I couldn't find a seat in my own car. Drank up all my liquor. Nobody spoke because we couldn't fix what happened. Evil silence.

I've lived a life
but nothin' I've gained.
Each day I'm filled
with sorrow and pain...

"Everybody out of my car."

"Please Bessie. We know how you feel."

"Out of my damn car! You don't know shit about my feelings. Get the 'f' out. Were you there when them railroad men thought I'd come to clean his floors? That's right, the day I bought my own railroad car."

"Maud, where my gun?"

"You don't have a gun, Bessie."

"I'm gone get one for me, you, and Clarence, and when I say 'Shoot'..."

"We won't miss," the trumpet man said.

"Is that supposed to be funny?" I said.

"I'm just playing, Bessie."

"That girl...didn't have a chance... if we could have been there, we could have kept her alive. Right, Maud?"

"Bessie, drink this. It will settle your nerves. There's nothing we can do. It's miles away."

"No it ain't. It's right here with us. You know it and I know it and what we gonna do?"

"Bessie, don't break that window. It can't bring the girl back. You don't even know her name."

Before long we all were down on the floor in our cups, drinking ourselves to sleep. No amazement, only rage. Plenty of reasons to keep watch on the lone prairie. Couldn't convince myself I was rich after that because being rich used to conquer sadness. I bit my lip and let the blood flow. Sky and land. Racket of wheels, hours to Houston and no sleep. Did it happen or was it just bad brew? Nobody dared bring it up again. For the rest of the tour, smiles were strictly for the show. Back in Chattanooga, Mr. Outlaw used to say, "When life's not worth living, the end's a blessing."

Is that what the girl in the tree thought? That at least she didn't have this cruel Texas to hope in?

Chapter 21

It was so hot in Concord, North Carolina, the leaves dripped like rags. Only rocks didn't care. Brick stacks puffed smoke and animals hid in the shade. Just to wake up was to be defeated. I hollered for ice to soak my tongue. Staying inside the Pullman wasn't much better than facing the daylight. When I raised the shade, the sun put a sword in my eye. The sky full of dead clouds.

I spent the day in panties and a slip until Clarence made me wear a kimono to talk business. I couldn't understand the problem but he said it's too hot for a parade. I guess he forgot squares don't like change.

"The sun sets every night," was my answer.

We worked the street like any day. Trumpet players' lungs, guitar picker's fingers skated off the fret board, and makeup ran. The town got what it expected.

The magician had an itchy ear, a sure danger sign for him in the shuffle trick. His memory was a swamp. He pointed to sweaty field our tent was staked on. The darkness was too deep, a pitiful few lightning bugs.

"One night is like another one. Get sober by show time," I said to the crew.

Evening brought the town off their porches and into our hands. We sold out the benches in twenty minutes. Our roustabouts kept the no accounts and kids from sneaking even a free peek. I gave away ten tickets in a drawing but I was tight on the money. Clarence roped off a "white" section although he thought it wasn't necessary.

"Nobody's gonna say nothing out here but it's your show," he said.

The tent was divided by a big center aisle. Two white guys sat on |opposite sides of the aisle so blacks could only have the rows behind them. Clarence asked them to please sit in one section on one side.

They ignored him. Clarence roped off the dividing line at the tenth row to please them but the white boys left when the show started.

The slack wire act and the magician were nearly through when the footlights failed. A car backfired. The magician fell to the floor and made it look like part of the act. The comedy team worked hard for skimpy laughs. The crowd soured. They'd paid their money and still felt miserable. Lights failed again, the generator wheezed more heat into the tent. I was singing *Nashville Women really ain't no bluff* when the trumpet man split. I'd get him told. He said later that the rat-a-tat sound of the dancers made him sick. Nobody leaves me in the middle of a tune. I wore a satin gown with real pearls, a white ostrich plume on a beaded cap, Paris stockings and perfect shoes. I don't play down to the tents. I wear the same stuff on Broadway. After the last bow, I cued the band to blow one without me and went on out. The trumpet player was crouched down close to the side flap.

"What you mean, crapping out of the tune?" I said. He covered my mouth with his hand and pointed to the back of the tent.

"Look what they're doing. KKK's pulling the tent down. They're trying to kill somebody."

I circled to the other side and told the roustabouts to follow me. Since they were always beating on each other, they might be good for something after all. I was in the lead, tiptoeing toward the digging. The hatchet headed fools were pulling my tent stakes up like carrots when I asked what the fuck they were doing. The biggest one was just out of reach, the night moonless and flat. I told my boys to come on but they stumbled on a snake in the grass and was too scared to step over it.

"Pick a brick and kill it," I said but they didn't have but two hands.

Long stripes of light leaked from the tent. The trumpet man said a noise like a gator crushing bones rushed from my belly. I told the white sheets they'd be safer sucking a wolf's dick than messing with my tent. There were eight of them, two big as Jack. Squares of lantern light flared across my body. The closest boll weevil moved back. I charged, head down but they were already running away. A crowd ran out of the tent to see. I pointed to cars with no lights speeding away.

"That's the Ku Klux Klan running from Bessie Smith."

I expected the black folk to shake my hand and have a big laugh but they they hesitated.

"I ain't scared," I said to the black and the white. "Somebody tell me why the Ku Klux Klan can't handle the blues?"

* * *

I made the spineless tent boys pound the pegs in deep and replace the cut ropes. The flaps opened wide to let the night take over.

Next two months booked solid through Georgia and Alabama, then on to Dallas and start to work our way back home. Everybody knows I love my fun but I don't play regarding my show. We're known as the best of the best, sold out shows, year after year. Audiences expected us to be Harlem sharp and I demanded it every night. Nobody slides with me. Know your steps or pack your bags. This white stage manager in Houston fucked up the scene changes. My dancers almost tripped over props he was supposed to take off stage. Instead of paying attention to business he's talked to his wife like they are at home with nothing to do. I broke into their conversation to get things straight. He gave me some lip like I was nobody, so I cold cocked him and said "Do your job." He was quiet as a lamb after that. I am the damn star and who the fuck did he think he was?

Soon as the show was over, Ruby came crying.

"Bessie, you have to get out of here."

"What you mean? I haven't even got my makeup off."

"That stage manager is dangerous. You can't do him and his wife like that. This isn't New York."

"Leave me alone, Ruby. Keep your pants dry."

"Bessie, I'm waiting for you. We're leaving together."

"Suit yourself."

The usual flunkies and backstage johnnies surrounded me.

"Bessie, loved the show. You've never been better. Come over and meet one of your biggest fans. I'm serious. He's got all your records," the manager said.

"Bessie, we got to go," Ruby said.

"They want me to autograph some records. I'm going to the parking lot."

They had a big Packard, my favorite car. The door swung out, I bent down to take a pen from a hand but was pulled in. I thought they wanted money but the motherfuckers just wanted to curse and slap me. The car peeled off, my legs dangled out the door. They beat on me speeding through town. I could have slid out of the door. You know I fought but they were too big. Raced through Houston calling me every kind of nigger.

I'd be dead if Ruby hadn't flagged a police car and found them whipping me in a vacant lot. Think the police arrested the bastards that left me bloody and disgusted? Teeth loose, talking to myself.

Only Maud didn't hold back her tongue.

"Bessie, you rich but don't own the world. Same people who had it yesterday still got it. It would have been worse if Ruby hadn't seen them"

"The police chased the car but they took their time," Ruby said.

"Of course, they did. Those deputies knew who the men were. They were all in on it. Crackers love to hear Bessie sing but she insulted that white woman and they couldn't allow that. Not down South. Not even Bessie can be that free," Maud said. She cleaned my face and arms, picked sticks and leaves from my hair. I refused a hospital visit, finished the tour, pretended nothing happened.

140

Chapter 22

Carl Van Vechten was a New York white man in love with Negroes. Some might criticize that, but I think it's too bad there's not more like him. He wrote nice things about me, liked jazz and "snow" in after-hours Harlem with friends like my piano player, Porter Grainger. Van Vechten had invited me to a society party and I decided to go between shows. Ruby and I wore matching ermine with Porter as our escort. Van Vechten and his wife met us in the marble vestibule that led to their big shot apartment with window sills deep enough to sit in. Big crowd of people. I heard Fred Astaire and Gershwin were there but didn't see them. The maid's silver tray stayed full of cold martinis, a black butler shook ice cubes and smiled. Cold cuts made me thirsty but the whiskey was prime, no bite, only gloss. An opera singer did her stuff by the big piano, loud enough to shake the view. I told her she was first class.

"Bessie, remember you got three more shows today," Porter said between conversations. I didn't appreciate being second guessed. I don't get drunk early unless I'm off tour and worried. I felt good but there were too many white folk waiting for me to speak first.

"Miss Smith, can I get you anything? Please call me Carlo," Van Vechten said. "Would you consider favoring us with one or two of your wonderful blues songs?"

I asked for another drink. Porter started the intro before I could get across the room good. I walked carefully because I hate to let good liquor spill. The crowd's ears were full of opera but I laid *Downhearted Blues* on them. The help peeped around kitchen doors; the prissy butler tapped his foot. Good as the opera singer was, I hit a pool of broken notes that made her performance disappear. My world and Central Park are two different things. I did two or three numbers but was pissed because Porter rushed the time on *Careless Love*. I told him to follow, not lead, and Van Vechten's friends gave that tickled kind of chuckle they think is cute. I cut off the show because Ruby was pointing to her watch while dragging my furs on the floor. I yelled for her to mind my property. Van Vechten's wife, who I wasn't talking to, said the floor had been washed that morning.

I stared her down, a woman with a foreign-sounding voice, who was just bigger than a dwarf. Porter had my arm, though I didn't need steadying, while he led me toward the door. I remember a huge pot of flowers, too many people waved goodbye. I felt overheated, a strange food smell about made me puke. I told Porter to stop rushing me. Van Vechten kissed my hand talking about "jazz spirituals," everything alright until his wife mumbled "goodbye," dug her nails in my neck, then smooched me like we're lovers.

"Don't be kissing me," I said. "Ain't this some shit."

I shook her off and let her fall to that clean floor she was bragging about. The crowd took a deep breath like I hit her though she was up in a minute! I wasn't apologizing. Why couldn't his woman shake hands like she was normal? If she'd acted right, nothing would have happened. The crowd surrounded her with baby talk, cutting their eyes at me.

Van Vechten followed Porter and me out of the door saying it was "all a misunderstanding," almost two sounds at once. Porter said I'd set the "race" back ten years. I sprayed the hall with curses. The elevator man couldn't get us out of the building fast enough. I said fuck him in his ass and twice on Sunday.

"Dammit Bessie," Clarence said when Ruby and I waltzed back stage at the Lafayette Theater. Hot coffee and cold compresses sobered me enough to work.

I still had a big time payroll, every record a hit. Offers to sing in California like "Long Goody" Ethel Waters but why cross the desert to make the same money I could get in Memphis?

I was cheap with wages but generous about teaching others how to be a pro. Skip my show if you only want half-white bitches because I hire my color first. Folk whisper because Jack Jr. is light-complexioned like I couldn't love him, but I don't hate nobody's skin. I hate *dicty* fancy Negroes who think somebody's color is better than mine.

Hit all the Toby Time theaters with "Mississippi Days." *Empty Bed Blues* moved plenty butts out of their cribs to see me. I had forty-five people to pay but my pocketbook stayed fat. Two thousand a week plus profits from peanuts, crackerjack, trinkets. Two hundred dollars every time I cut a record. The safe was too heavy to carry before three weeks passed. Grueling hours between cities were clubbed to death by success.

A week later, I called about Snooks and Jack admitted Viola was doing her part. We promised to try again. His answers cradled my ear in Arkansas, soft as pillows. I love pleasure too much and want to forget too quick. The days were smooth and calm but the wild sound was in my ear again. I changed clothes and should have stayed in my stateroom, while the big Pullman carried me like the Empress they said I was. I showed Duke and Basie how to carry their people so Jim Crow can't touch them. I never asked to be royalty but I didn't object.

It was exercise walking from one end of the car to the other or down to the deep galley. I had safe company at my table but I still went to the new girls' compartment. Just had to see them playing cards, laughing in pajamas and robes, drinking nighttime voices that whispered low. That new one, Ruby's friend, returned my smile but I should have let it go by. I spent too much time with her while the others were around. It was too easy to have her visit and Ruby to leave. It was too easy to find the ways to congratulate her on not very much and of course she was impressed with all my name advertised. I let rolling wheels and the nightfall destroy promises I swore. Couldn't stop my hands from wanting and there was no reason strong enough to stop me. Gossip said she was "in the life" but I had no proof yet. If Ruby was jealous, she didn't complain and stayed useful turning up clues. When I get excited about new love, my face can pimple up from eating too much sugar. Just making conversation has caused my breath to shorten and wheeze.

"You been on the road long?" my opening line. I started corny because there was so much about her I didn't know.

"Near five years."

"How you like it so far?"

"Beautiful, Miss Bessie. This is better than I thought."

I moved closer; she didn't back up. I knew others were watching so my hands stayed on the table. Not that I cared, but timing is everything.

"I'm going to keep an eye out for you," I said. "You sing?"

"Thank you, Miss Smith."

"I'm Bessie. Just plain Bessie. Call me that from now on."

"I....I don't know what to say."

"Don't say, just do and not boo-hoo. Is that a promise?"

Her turn to get shy and I let her squirm. Her pouty breasts. My satin doll. She clung but knew when to sleep by herself. Because of that, I took her places that I might not take others. Buy her something she never thought she would have. Taxi to a girl's club after the show asking, "You been here before?" knowing damn well what the answer was.

"No, but I heard about it," Doll said.

I laughed because she was always right with the drift.

Satin Doll was discreet as a thief. She didn't steal because I gave whatever she wanted. Her lips reminded me of evenings when the world began but by the weekend, there was nothing new left to see.

Chapter 23

At the beginning of '29 I realized there was such a thing as too much success because I had to keep track of it. Money from tours, advances, radio shows, souvenirs and refreshments at the tents. Without Maud and Clarence, the whole thing would have gone bust.

"Jack Gee? This is Sam Reevin, Theater Owners Booking Association, here. Bessie's been cleaning up all year. Most of the other acts are dying but she's still hot. Orchestras and movies are the new tip. Still a chance for a high-class performer though. I'd like you to produce two shows for the first of the year."

"Bessie, the Toby Time theater owners want a new show for January. That's word for word. You'll have to front me three thousand to get ready. You have any problem with it?" Jack said.

I agreed to rehearse the cast but all the other details were his. I'd take Jack Jr. on tour until spring break. My spirits flew too high. The world looked clean. Jack and I just celebrated our fifth anniversary but we were like a screen door hanging off the frame. Maybe he thought that money came natural because I made it look too easy. He had heard about hard times but never lived mine. Maybe he needed worries and I could only see the bookings ahead. I believed money could cure all problems because I hadn't had any until I was grown. Bullshit could have been diamonds.

I couldn't resist making the boy happy. I bought him clothes only a doctor's child could have. Tried to make up for all the days I had to be gone.

Snooks woke when I was barely asleep so I had to hand him off to Maud, then to make up for that I'd buy him presents. I guess that was the start of him believing he'd always get what he wanted. Toys, books, fine today, forgotten tomorrow. Then he'd miss his Mama, crying terrible when the train was hours from a phone. I couldn't blame him, but worried because she might want him back.

"Why we have to travel so long? Where are other kids to play with? Why, Why, Why?"

I got tired saying "I don't know" but it was like having little Bud again when Snooks fell asleep in my arms. That's when my hope climbed highest. If he could sing or dance I'd put him the show. He'd get his schooling though. Believe that we'd see to that. He could be a lawyer and represent me with the record companies or a doctor to heal the sick. Maybe invent something precious. He'd be so smart no prejudice could keep him down. His eyes could melt the ice between Jack and me. We put down our curses, got peaceful because of the boy in his sailor suit, the blocks saying "G for Goose, P for Pear." Sheltered him like magnolia leaves, all disappointment refused.

"S'pose we get lucky and have our own child," Jack said.

"No use getting our hopes up," I said.

"I didn't say it would happen, I said, 's'pose.'"

"S'pose we stay happy if we don't. Is that okay, baby?"

"Sure, baby. No harm in dreaming. Right? Where would you be if there'd been no dreaming?"

Coming to agreement after weeks of cold hearts was like finding a window where a wall use to be. The child thought he was close enough to touch the sun when he sat on Jack's shoulders. I had no shows for three weeks, nothing to do but live. Of course it couldn't last. I loved Snooks but I was relieved to give him back to Viola and hit the road again.

I worked "Steamboat Days" January and February, east coast to Cleveland to turn away business. Talked with Jack real regular at the beginning of the tour but he suddenly got unavailable. I figured he'd gone fishing. I even disappointed the bootleggers by staying on the wagon, concentrated on giving my best onstage and cutting up with Ruby. After several weeks being perfect, decided I could be a little naughty and crossed over to the Kentucky side for some liquor. Ruby acted strange after talking with a young guy at the club.

"It's getting late, Bessie. We gotta go now to make the curtain."

"We got plenty of time. Somebody on the horizon?"

"We really should go."

The fellow handed me a trade paper:

JACK GEE'S NEW SHOW WITH BROWN SKIN BEAUTY
GERTRUDE SAUNDERS OPENED IN COLUMBUS.

I read it several times while Ruby hung her head. The boy asked me what the show was about but I left before I hurt him. I read the article three or four times to be sure I really understood on the ride back to Cleveland.

The heat of the makeup lights soothed me. My reflection in the mirror belonged to a stranger. I should have started a fire in the dressing room. Think theater-owners care if we catch pneumonia? I ripped through the show, ran through the bows, thinking about what I'd say when I saw Jack, what he or I might do.

"We're going to Columbus," I said.

Ruby mumbled that we shouldn't go nowhere but we were at the curb lickety-split.

"Listen lady, sure you got the money?" I gave the cabbie twenty dollars and said "shut up until that was gone." Ruby pointed to one of my playbills on a wall. The cabbie read "Empress of the Blues" out loud and whistled. After that, he said "yes ma'am" to everything. His car smelled of burnt oil. Nothing to see but hills and phone poles. Ruby said we'd been with the new show over three weeks. I remembered Jack had chose to not spend a day with me all that time and we weren't but a overnight train away. I rolled the window down to puke. The cabbie pulled off the road saying the stuff will just blow in the car. Ruby wiped my mouth and held me. She said I was more kin to her than Jack would ever be. I thanked her but I didn't want to be reminded of his family.

When we got to the rooming house I had Ruby wait outside. Jack wasn't gonna be slick enough to find someplace new. I hoped Gertie opened the door because my first love tap would break her face and the next would knock her out. I was disappointed to see him but his surprise was worth the fifty dollars the cab cost.

147

"Jack, It's all over."

"Okay, I lied," he said.

"That makes us even."

"I'm working six shows a day like a beginner, and you're fucking Gertie on my dime."

"But it's all reet when you play. Isn't it?" he said.

"I play on my dime. You financed her show on the three thousand I fronted you first of the year."

"You agreed to it," he said, knowing I trusted him to build a second show for me.

I was at one end of a tunnel and him at the other.

"I love her more, Bessie. Love her like I once loved you." With each word I hated every promise, every kiss between us.

"Then why didn't you say that and been on your way?"

"I didn't know that I really loved Gertie until you went on the road this last time. I got so lonely I couldn't resist her. I intended to book both shows for you until she couldn't find a gig and asked for help."

I chuckled at the stupidity of his excuse. The ignorance of his nerve.

"Didn't I put your show together, the one that's making so much green?" he said, knowing Maud and Clarence had done almost everything except for the little bit they figured he couldn't fuck up.

"What's this got to do with that heifer?"

"She hasn't done nothing to you."

"Except steal my man?"

"You don't want me. You want whatever flits by. I stay home waiting for you but you don't wait for a streetcar, let alone me. Tell me I'm wrong. Besides, what happened to the idea that 'your money' was 'our money'?

Don't you remember about 'for better or for worse, richer or poorer?' That's what 'our money' means."

"So the money you stole is your pay?" I reasoned.

"I shouldn't have done it, but I figured to pay it back before you missed it."

"Things didn't work out, did they?" I said.

"Hadn't been for that article..."

"Tell the truth, Jack, you want her because she's so white-looking."

"Everything's a color with you," he said.

"Where you think we live?" I said.

"Gertie don't fool with another woman," he said.

"You get wet and sticky no matter what," I said.

"Can't tell me it's normal," he said.

"Did she look the other way when you had your fun?" I said.

"I ain't never been like you," he said.

Doesn't matter who hit first. I didn't care if I died. We slammed from one side of the hallway to the other. Somebody tried to open the door but Jack had me pinned.

"Gertie, get out of here. Crazy woman trying to get in."

I heard her Cinderella slippers flying away but one day she'll be mine. Jack bear-hugged and swarmed me but I slipped out the knot, ran into the bedroom hoping Gertie might be near enough to grab. Jack was right there. No escape but a window. The phone rang. Jack grabbed it.

"The police are coming," I heard the desk clerk say.

"She'll be dead before they get here," Jack said.

I believed him. He missed most of his punches but the bad one put a lot of blood in the sink.

"You don't care about nobody," we both said to the other.

"I love her," he admitted.

"Shut up and pay me my money," I said.

"Let me see your lip. Look what you made me do. This would never happen with Gertie. I want her because she's a lady,"

"And what does that make me?" I said.

His suit would never button again. Tore that room up. Jack and I waited for the cops.

"Miss Smith, we can't settle the bill until I've seen the premises," the weasel clerk said.

I gave him three hundred, then hired a cab to drive around until I sobered up. I couldn't remember if I had another week at the theater. If stores had been open, I'd have bought a year's worth of clothes. No more Bessie Smith Gee, just plain Bessie Smith. We crossed a bridge and the tears came rolling. Sudden cold light, water below, the years of fame like they happened to someone else.

* * *

"Did Uncle Jack ask about me?"

"I got the problem, not you," I said, but Ruby knew her family much better than me. She looked like she might cry. I told her to snap out of it because Jack wasn't going to break me down for more than a few days. I was going to drink and curse until my lips were sick of his name. That's why I made the department store clerks bring out ten pair of shoes at a time and dared them to make me wait. Sat with the society bitches in Baltimore and didn't ask for permission. A woman gave me her drink to hold but I let it fall.

"I ain't your mammy."

If she said something, I'd have put her ass on the floor. Stores treat me cool because I'm Bessie. I wink at the scared sisters sweeping up. I tipped the shine man ten dollars because he was fine. I told the sales girl, "I don't like that color" just to make her bite her tongue. I'll call the manager in a minute. They serve me tea on dishes they break an hour later. I ain't fooled. Big stores think they're "nice" by letting me try on a dress. If they get me on a bad day, I'll choose twenty gowns a size too small and bust out the seams.

Defaults, car notes, breach of contract came thick as snow. Jack closed bank accounts so I'd bounce checks. Even after he agreed to settle, he stood me up to have his fun.

To stay busy, I worked bullshit jobs with casts who met each other on opening night. The worse my situation with Jack got, the more Tinnie and Viola complained. The restaurant I bought for them was a sinkhole.

"We got to have more money, Bessie. The toilet backed up and the plumber didn't fix it. He's a gangster pretending to be a worker."

Why did I think adding a business onto their life would work? My ear was stitched to the phone but I hardly heard them. I'd bought them two houses because they fought so bad. They twisted around me like weeds.

I'd made much more money than I'd hoped for. By 1931, my blues were still in the penthouse, but the building had sunk a few floors. I promised my sisters they wouldn't want for nothing but I felt used and empty hearted. I didn't argue anymore. If they said one hundred dollars would fix it, I'd give seventy-five and leave. My nieces thought I was their grandmother. Tinnie figured begging babies would shake more money loose than she could. I said "Go back to Chattanooga" but "they didn't know nobody." Been raised there and now the "Jim Crow is too bad" like Philly was The Promised Land. I played Connie's Inn up in Harlem, but think I was welcome to sit and drink?

I lived for the road. Show me a stage door and hangers-on who'll do what I say. Then ordinary time don't figure. The empty halls beg me to blow smoke and I don't shortchange. I tell Cincinnati why grown men wake up crying. I don't know why I have to do this but I don't want nothing else.

* * *

151

Swing down Cadillac, let me ride.

My big girl had sheer love in her legs, put no frost on my windows. Being with her had the lazy pace of an empty day. Just Live, the sign on the bar read. Gladys Bentley's Clam House. Gladys played boogie woogie piano in top hat and tails. Mannish without apologies, ivory cigarette holder, she sang songs that made pimps blush. Patrons laughed themselves to tears, ashamed of having such a good time. All this without even going upstairs.

Marian caught my eye across the buffet table. We put our feelings where they wanted to be in no time. She gifted me with a key to her apartment. I loved to surprise her and often succeeded. Listened for footsteps light and fast as thoughts. When she discovered me in her bed wearing only a silk robe, saying, "Come and get it!" she beat her fists against me while I smelled her sweet sweat. I draped pearls between her breasts. Her legs made me swear Jack was going to be my last man. I loved her teeth, her breasts filled with honey milk, that sweet wax that made me come. She made me dizzy with her nonsense. She was like feathers down there.

Marian was a ladies girl but life stayed hard because of her beauty. She couldn't saunter 125th without a man assuming they had something to talk about.

"I'm a movie star without the money," she said without grief. "Seen you sing a lot of times."

"I thought you avoided big crowds," I said.

"Guys look past me when I'm not made up."

"If they only knew."

"I've had enough of that."

"If somebody lays a hand on you..."

"Don't protect me, Bessie. Just be sweet, have some laughs. The world is sad until somebody like you comes along. Don't make me into something I'm not. I don't stay attached very well."

152

"Are you telling me to go?" I said.

"You surprise me, Bessie."

"Really?"

"People think you're so rough but I see a lot of softness."

"I give what I get."

Marian moved closer. We kissed, made angel love, the kind nobody thinks they'll find.

"That's why I bring you things."

"I appreciate the gifts but I appreciate you more."

"You don't want the gifts?"

"They're not necessary but I love the intention."

"You're a strange one, Marian."

"Thanks for noticing."

"When will I see you again?"

"When are you next in Harlem?"

"Probably not for six weeks"

"Call Gladys, she will know where I am. And don't lose the key," she said.

* * *

I'm past proud and sassy, I'm a kingdom. It'll be my ruin because kings ain't aces. When gray skies captured me in the past, I made Jack take me to the fights. We watched the day laborers beat each other down but sat five rows back because blood shoots farther than you'd think. Blood don't thrill or scare me. A knockout punch can land any time, so do your best.

I finished the tour, made the theater-owners happy, filled my accounts with scratch. I was on time for most shows, wild as a storm, and so filled with feeling everybody knew that blues was my daily bread.

"You singin' your life, ain't you Miss Bessie?" said voices from the back.

"Hell, yes," I said. "Is your husband home alone?"

The musicians did their barnyard imitations while I ran the dancers. I told the new ones, loud enough for the audience to hear, they'd better learn steps fast as they get popular because I fire people who are out of date. I fought to the bell, ready to be the star when the music began. There are no secrets, every life starts and ends the same way. I don't care if the audiences hoot like owls because after a few minutes, they're going to hope the music never stops, even though they know it will. The world ain't much good, but if you're half-brave, you can make it seem grand.

Too bad love doesn't last. I'll never forget Jack pawned his uniform and watch so I'd look right at the first recording session. Shed a tear even now, when he's nothing to me. I took down the pictures of Jack and me carefully at first but there were holes in the walls before I was through. I stomped the smiling photos, cut out his picture from the pile of snapshots to make dolls that were folded and torn. Tried to empty his sugar voice from my head. I demanded the contact list that he'd taken from the office. I paid what he wanted for them when we met in the smelly lobby of Gertie's apartment building.

"Here it is," he said, handing over the books. I asked about Jack, Jr. He shook his head like it hurt.

"We promised his Mama the boy would be raised right and we don't even know where he is," I said.

"I didn't make him leave. Snooks is a big boy and if he thinks he can run off and handle it, let him try."

I worried that the boy would fall farther and deeper now that Jack and I had split. It looked like we had forgotten our dream about a baby we could rock and coo. Didn't Jack care about the phone call when Snooks first called him "Dad"?

I got famous while the boy's mother had babies because she believed in men who would never get a chance with me. I heard her admit she couldn't feed babies with ashes from the chimney. We reminisced about lost early days, then I promised to raise her baby because the Empress of the Blues had everything but a child.

Not long after I split with Jack, Ruby called.

"Bessie, listen. I can't talk long." Worry dripped off her whisper, tears in the words. "He won't let me travel with you no more. He's a dog, Bessie. He ain't my Daddy. I love you, Bessie."

Jack forced her off the line and hung up. He'd do anything to make me blue. He knew I'd taught Ruby the business, even let her sing sometimes and didn't make her do anything she didn't already want.

The phone rang again.

"Stay way from Ruby, hear? I'm Ruby's family and we're through with you."

Jack stung his words through the line, bit them short.

"Why can't she speak for herself? You told me to take her on the road."

"I wanted somebody to check on you," he said.

"You saying she's a spy?"

"It's one in the p.m. and you just got up, didn't you? Alcohol for breakfast and who's in the bed with you? One of your street girls or a boy you trying to turn back?"

"Let me talk to Ruby."

"She's too good for you. What happened to my manager fees?"

He cut me off in mid curse.

Instead of roaring back, I poured a drink, cooked neck bones and rice with a clear and untroubled mind. Turned on the box, Ethel Waters crooned while I ironed and drank the afternoon away. It was dark when

I drew my bath but I was too high to step in. Soaked my feet in the tub, and hoped Ruby would be alright.

Next morning I found one of Jack's guns in a shoe box. I unwrapped it like a present, and thought about all I could do with it. I counted out the heavy bullets, imagined Gertie and Jack begging mercy like I was God.

Ruby met me downtown a week later. We sat in a park while she cried about being forced to work with Gertie.

"It ain't half fair, Bessie. Let me come back. They aren't any fun."

Her pleading touched me.

"I'm not even sure Gertie knew it was your money Jack was spending until I told her. She's meaner to Jack than you were. She hurts him with high class words, mocks him because he can hardly read. You're the real star."

I cried with her but knew Jack wouldn't let her go. A hard slap would've helped but I didn't have the heart.

"Be sweet and and keep your legs closed, Ruby. Nothing lasts."

❦ Chapter 24 ❦

Around 1930, Richard Morgan and I met again in Chicago. He had that eager look, so I accepted his invitation to go out. It wasn't dramatic or heroic. We were almost ordinary.

"You following me, handsome?"

"It's a free country."

"They ain't meaning us," I said.

"What about us?" he said.

"You tell me," I said.

"I don't want to move too fast."

"That's real gentlemanly but you don't want to take it too slow neither."

"I can do it fast, slow, in between," he said.

"I bet you can" I said.

"Long as it ain't no trap."

"You're a businessman," I said.

"That loves good music. Especially yours."

"I appreciate how you took care of me in Chicago back when."

"We have history, Bessie. What do you say?"

After a week of fireworks in bed, I asked Richard where this was going.

"Going until you say stop."

I expected him to change once he knew me better, but Richard's way was to offer help before being asked. He even got along with the family. When Viola whined, he listened like he was interested. If the icebox got bare, a grocery boy showed up with boxes of food. Don't even mention liquor; it was common as water since he was making it undercover.

Toby Time went bust in 1930. Took down so many of the black companies with it but the Depression didn't make a big difference for me. Good as it was, *Black Mountain Blues* only pressed a few thousand copies but the Mobile, New Orleans, Dallas circuit still paid in spite of more empty seats than last year. Richard said cut the payroll in half, no more than fifteen or twenty.

By 1931, I'm still in business and that's saying a lot. Richard lowered my fee down into the seven hundreds, thought it better to stay closer to home, concentrate on Philly theaters like the Standard and the Pearl. Fifty cents is a lot of money but my fans still paid for what I had to offer.

"Hello Bessie, this is Walker. Got studio time booked for November 20th. Rehearse your band and let's spread some rhythm on wax."

I knew the scene had changed direction since the last sessions. I leaned toward swing, rushed the beat, moved from furs to summer frocks. I was thirty-five, in my prime, and figured Walker was on the trend, ready for me to shift gears. I'd had a decent year despite the talkies wrecking the traveling shows. I took second bill to a few flicks but the big bands were getting most of the play. Only my name saved me from striking out.

Walker and Clarence had booked a helluva tour through the South though we lost our ass in Texas. I lowered prices, kept a full cast by promising a bonus at the end of the tour. The pay was low but they'd be pros when I was done with them.

The late November Columbia session started okay, but a draft was blowing.

"Walker, how you like the new stuff?"

He sat straight with just a blink of excitement while we romped and stomped.

"It's up to date, Bessie. I like it, but..."

"But... it's too slow. Maybe needs more pep. Okay, no problem. It has to be copacetic." I said, finishing his thought for him.

"Don't get ahead of me. Copacetic? What is that?"

"It means the 'best' Walker. Why ain't you hep?"

"Bessie, business is bad. You're not a hep chick, you're the Empress of the Blues. We're lucky to cut a thousand recordings. You're not selling fifty thousand, hell, not even fifteen any more."

"What are you saying, Walker? Nothing wrong with being hep. The houses stay full on my tours. The country is going to hell but folk still like to hear Bessie. I'm on the scene and know what to do."

"Do like the song says, Bessie: Safety First."

"Walker, the street's dropping the blues like measles. Audiences get up in the slow songs, the same ones that used to break their hearts."

"You're the blues if anyone is. Don't forget what built you. I want that down home Bessie beat. This is not the time to trot out a new Bessie."

I tapped my foot in hopes a new rhythm might reach him. His forehead wrinkled in pain. I noticed that he packed his own bottle this time. His overcoat was out of style. I told my boys to take five. He poured me one and lit a cigar. The studio felt refrigerated, the ceilings cloud high, every sound too bright and extended. There was no gossip or plans for the next tour. I tipped the glass to let the heat flow on down.

"Alright Walker, I'll stick with you, but next time promise we'll try something new."

"See you tomorrow, Bessie."

I knew my direction was right but Walker was no dummy. He knew the blues was hot when other whites played it cheap. I'd try his way but change was everywhere. The theaters didn't want a stage show by itself any more. I had to compete with a movie for top billing and couldn't afford to hire a full cast any more. It was true that I still had decent attendance, but after the '29 crash, the music scene drove with its brakes on.

"Walker's lost faith in the business," was how Richard explained it. "Good thing you know yourself."

159

The next day Walker was shaved and pressed, acted more like himself. I buried worry and roared into the groove. I predicted crowds would eat up the new tunes, hungry for my butt-shaking girls. I was full of plans, ready to work.

"Bessie, there isn't going to be a next time for awhile."

I didn't say nothing, my mind empty, the room hardly there. He took another drink without wiping his mouth.

"I'm sorry but there's nothing I can do. They gave me the word last night. Columbia's cancelled you and a lot of others. You'll get a severance check in a few days for the unused sessions on the contract and we'll have to call it a day. We've had some good times, haven't we, Bessie? You are the greatest. No doubt in anybody's mind. The country's gone to hell. Not my fault, not yours."

"I sold more records than anybody, Walker. Deny it."

"Columbia, me and nobody else denies your success, Bessie. You are the greatest. No question. Good things come to an end. People aren't buying anything. Even your great sides stay on the shelf because people got to eat."

"I told you it was time to do a swing record."

"It was out of my hands. They told me to give you up."

"Columbia Records said give me up? Did you remind them I'm the Empress of the Blues?"

"I don't count, Bessie. They tell me, I don't tell them."

"Ain't this a bunch of shit. Hmmm? Well. I don't dwell on the bad news. The east coast never loved me like the South," I said.

"I understand you're angry. Don't you see bread lines everywhere? Nobody knows what's going to happen. This is a terrible situation."

I shook Walker's hand but didn't take a drink like I usually would have.

The news crushed me but I stayed light on my feet. That was it. No more notes or drop ins. No calls or staying in touch. It was like a romance gone bad. I didn't need Columbia to prop me up. Richard knew without asking because I was already drunk when he got home.

"Don't worry, baby. Let me take care of the details. Get your show ready. Long as the South Side stays thirsty, there will be funds to invest."

The next day I checked the warehouse where my props and costumes were stored. Two years earlier the place would have been bustling. I stayed strong. Walker thought he had it figured but forgot I had done more business than five dance bands. The mirrors whispered I still looked good. Bessie's blues don't need a vacation.

I had gotten used to the ripped up look of the glory places; boarded up, stripped and shameless. The Depression prowled Philly and New York like Dracula. Not just black folks pinched pennies. Everybody cringed when they had to give up change for groceries. It was worth an hour's walk to save a quarter. A tide of black faces owned the avenues Saturday night, far from the stoves, docks and tubs that held them tight. I gave satisfaction to the dissatisfied including myself because I knew what a hot horn can do. We preached syncopation, played through the ass beatings and let blue moods rule the world. I was taught that females were smarter than men but we rolled on floors too, beating each other ragged with a purse. Some folk think I don't care about love because I sing the blues, but it's just the opposite. I search for love like a convict praying for a pardon. You can't give me somebody else's baby once I had my own.

Remember when the apron under my dress stuffed with hundreds, fifties and thousand dollar notes wasn't nothing? By 1932 even the street lights bent low and poor. The department stores still dressed the windows but folks admired them like a play they'd never see.

I got famous following the space between things. Laugh if you want to. The world isn't simple, it's a thread that weaves a coat and a dress if you can see it. I followed Andrew to Ninth Street because he heard opportunity calling. It said, "Andrew, go get Bessie and bring her to the soft dust streets where tall windows are filled with shoes and black

dresses fine as spider's lace. Watch your own reflection, be at the exact spot to see ten light bulbs become a kind of lightning you can depend on."
Now that I've had everything, a dry taste keeps the sweet away. Wondering interrupts my dreams, the ordinary noises make a new language.
I talk to empty rooms but don't feel lonely. I'm partying but the voices fade down to whispers.

Since Columbia Records paid me out, so many think I'm through. When I walk by, conversation stops because I was once on top. If we go to clubs, musicians don't always ask me to sit in because I'll prove them weak. Microphones are no protection. I'll sing from the heart and no one will care what the others play. My tones shine so hard it shames them. I feel ears against my lips when singers try to copy me. Swing ain't new, it's what I left on my plate. Fast rhythm can't lose me, slow time is my meat. I keep the weight of clouds around my soul. When the weather turns bad, I'm ready. Been soaked in a flood, got burnt on the sunny side. Empty handed and yet won the prize, dead broke with a diamond wristwatch. Roll me and watch me stand. I sing to the center of things, to the meaning of each pitch.

Richard and I went for breakfast and had to walk in the street because the soup line was four deep, several blocks long.

"I can't eat with so many begging," I said.

"They'd eat and leave you in line. Please don't give out your change," Richard said. "We'll be here for hours and still half of them will want more than you have."

"The world's closing down. Maybe I should have gone overseas. Alberta Hunter and Ethel Waters still raising hell over there," I said.

"You'll have to go without me. I'd lose everything if I left town.." Richard said.

"You could import hooch wholesale, be a big syndicator."

"I could try, but Capone said prohibition is about over. I've got to get my business tight enough to survive booze going legit."

I wondered if this was Richard's way of saying goodbye. My hand had been in his pocket for years. He had peeled off bread for rent, groceries and clothes. He had a wife and baby across town we never talked about. His wife came to the front door once. She begged me to let him go but whose blues was that? The second act of my career wouldn't have happened without Richard Morgan. Who knows why he loves me. He could have anybody but says I'm his "Queen of the Nile."

1932 nearly broke me down though I never said it to anyone. Even if it's the end, I'm playing my hand. The morning's still sweet, my steps quick as a youngster's. I'm not afraid of the new thing. Billie Holiday sings a good microphone but I never feared the back row couldn't hear me. Me and Louis Armstrong are in her singing. Something about me holds attention. Alberta Hunter, Ethel Waters, Mamie Smith need last names to be remembered. I don't have that problem. Spell B-E-S-S-I-E, and that's all needs be said.

A good night's rest got hard to find. I woke Richard because I thought a spotlight was turned up full beam. He was tired of my nightmares but he'd get up and play cards with me. Sometimes we drove from Philly to New York just to clear our minds. I would roll down the windows and sing all through Harlem. People ran to the car at stoplights. I kissed babies like a politician. Just the night and the fame; minutes that cost no one anything.

Even in the Great Depression, the whole country on its knees, I don't give up. If my name's out front, it's worth your money. The beat the is soul of a song so let me take you to a thrill. I miss the glory days but don't need pity. Just hope to be half what I am.

So much has been taken. The hours mock hope and only the past lives. I don't hide my need to be noticed. I visit clubs I used to rule and dare the owners to ignore me. The brave ones talk past me and the other kind I curse. I remind them of the profits I created. My mouth is a tabulator. I mention their girlfriend's name and recall the dates we shared on Easy Street. I mention the diamond ring, their first new car. I never sing for free but I'll sing on a corner before I'll beg for a gig.

Don't believe those stories about me waiting tables and turning tricks. I was never last.

Back in Harlem, I turned out the Christmas crowd at the Lafayette. Nothing but raves and lots of butts in seats. Every gig was another chance to prove my worth.

I heard Ma Rainey gave up the road, bought a theater in Georgia and started to preach gospel. She wrote that she was content serving others. She didn't miss the blues; didn't need nothing but the Lord. I missed her, though. The Songbird was the true vine, a tap root for songs you haven't heard yet.

Some say the blues died about 1933, but I'm still Queen of the Blues. Roosevelt defeated Hoover and they say Prohibition is going out. My name may be in smaller letters but I was back at the Lafayette raising hell. The railcar and the big shows are gone, but what else do I know to do? Being seen used to guarantee work but when the whole country strips its gears, nobody's safe. I never waited for a miracle and won't start now.

A young white boy named John Hammond came to Philly and pitched a record deal. He was rich, smart and loved jazz. He had caught my act in Harlem about five years before.

"Miss Smith, you are America's greatest voice."

"Yes, that's what some say. Thank you."

"Jazz and blues are the same thing. I can get a recording date for you. It will take awhile but trust me."

"Let's not trust. Let's stay in touch," I said.

"I mean it. A lot of great musicians want to be on the record."

"You going to pay for it?" I said.

"Yeah, I'm good for it. It's my plan to bring in the best Negro and white musicians together to back you up playing solid blues."

"People want the snap and shuffle of swing now."

"I believe blues is the great American music. You're gonna hear from me."

I thanked him but thought he was looking backward, like Walker at Columbia. I was already up to date.

* * *

I hoped Jack Jr. was all right. He shouldn't want for anything, but he strayed so far from me. Nobody makes just one mistake when love withers, it's a fool's playhouse. Ain't it sad how the boy ran away headstrong and foolish in his good clothes? Maud and Clarence searched. Tinnie and Viola said they looked and maybe they did. Jack didn't care for Snooks but making me blue gave him happiness. After the boy got arrested several times, the judge said I traveled too much to be his guardian. Jack told the court I didn't care if Snooks was a truant. The judge ordered the boy to stay with Viola in Philly, but he still ran until he was caught and sent to a Wayward Boys Home. Ruby found out the boy had contacted Jack, thinking his step-dad would take him. Instead, Jack put our boy in military school and let me believe the Snooks was still lost. It all came down.

"Big as I've been, they don't want to give me a chance," I said.

"You're still big," Richard said, pinching my waist.

Hammond came through with the recording in New York City, November '33. I had four songs written in a swing style and a band with Frankie Newton, Jack Teagarden, Chu Berry, Benny Goodman even. Some of the best stuff I ever did. *Give Me a Pigfoot, Down In the Dumps, Do Your Duty, Take Me for a Buggy Ride.* Five years before, they would have been smash hits. Hell of it was that Okeh balked on releasing them! Hammond talks about a tour, gigs downtown.

Club-owners reminisced and promised they'd stay in touch but I wasn't waiting for their call. My name commanded table number one, so nobody could say I was hard to find. Richard trucked so much Prohibition hooch into the cabarets, it was always open door for us. His new plan was to keep producing unsealed hooch now that Prohibition was finished. I wasn't the only one who preferred unsealed! He knew how to survive as a bootlegger and saw no future in going legit, then being refused a license because it was a white man's racket.

My new pals, Mildred Bailey and Red Norvo, the swing stars, reminded me that talent like mine can get disorganized and run over, but it's still gold.

They worked the hippest scenes on 52nd Street so I figured the way to shake up the competition was to drop in a jam session and bring the swing crowd up to date on their own turf.

Richard and I read the autographs at the entrance to the Famous Door then climbed the stairs. Mildred told the announcer just to call my name. My piano player was ready with *Smoke Gets In Your Eyes*, *Get Happy*, *Sweet Georgia Brown*; a total change from the old days. I wore my cloche hat, a black shift, diamond necklace, hair brushed straight back.

"Give me that smile," Richard said.

I stepped onto the tiny stage, its low ceiling pushing down, laid the tempo medium up. Jaws dropped, eyes met mine, the kitchen help stood with mixing bowls in their hands. Hipsters who couldn't remember anything but their connections' phone numbers got happy about something new. I barely let them applaud, pressed on like opera, everything "downtown" and bittersweet then left them wanting more. Mildred refused to follow my act though her records were red hot.

"I got way better sense than that," she said.

Richard and I strolled under billboards that begged for better days.

"You got the goods no matter what the tune. Lionel Hampton, Goodman, Basie, all the cats are begging to record with you," he said.

"It's a sure thing," I said.

"Nobody knows how famous you're going to be this time."

"Hammond said he's lined me up to be featured in a *Jazz at the Philharmonic* concert somewhere. Strictly swing, no blues. Coming soon."

"Just a matter of scheduling," Richard said.

"I want to make another movie. That St. Louis Blues movie was too short. No chorus this time, my own people like a real stage show. No more of me crying on the bar stool over a slick fool."

"Should be a whole movie about you, a show that tells the real story of an artist."

"Think Hollywood wants to see back of the tracks?" I laughed.

"They'd have done it already if they were slick," Richard said.

I felt my heart singing to itself. A bubbling up like spring. Clouds were going home.

* * *

It was early but the tents and lean-tos beneath bridges already glowed. The smell of burned beans, smoke and clanging trains cut conversation off. Turned-up collars didn't protect the ears of worried girls. Big shouldered young men tramped and smoked, bitter as slaves.

"How long until we fall off the train ourselves?" I said, suddenly worried again.

"We're not about to fall off. People will buy liquor even if it means giving up pussy."

"Are you saying that between alcohol and women, I gotta lose?"

"Don't matter baby, you'll never do without," he said.

I guess passersby wondered what in the hell there was to laugh about, but we couldn't help ourselves. Dancing kept my steps Savoy light. I could Truck, Black Bottom, and Shimmy, anything except acrobatics. I loved helping orchestras shake the floors. Richard didn't dance but he wasn't jealous. I always had some gay boys to roll with, some ladies to greet. Of course I get low, the blues rises like a tide but look from where I came. Think there's no scars on the famous?

After all those years of five, six shows a night, Philly to St. Louis, anybody think I'm not a sure thing? Chick Webb! Bless his crippled self, nearly died every night beating those skins. They played high-speed blues gone to college swinging hard.

When I find Jack Jr., I'll never let him go. Hope he's learned the world don't care. It's a miracle when somebody wants you, a fountain of stars that don't go dim.

"Ruby, this is Bessie."

I know who it is.

"How are you doing?'

"You know damn well I ain't supposed to talk to you."

"I just wanted to hear your voice."

"Thought you was scared to disobey Jack."

"You're drunk, Bessie."

"Don't you want to be too?"

"Of course but I can't leave without Uncle Jack finding out."

"You saying that New York City is too small to get lost in?"

"I'm not bold as you. Just leave it alone for now. We'll have a ball like the old days sometime," she said.

"When will that be? Will I still be living? Will you?"

"This is Jack, Bessie. Hang up the damn phone. Leave my niece alone."

"She's no baby."

"Compared to you she is."

"Shut up, Jack. You heard from Snooks? You promised he would call me."

"Who knows when? He'll call when he can."

"Have you seen him? Is he doing his lessons?"

"Far as I know."

"Why did you turn him against me?"

"I didn't do anything."

"Gertie pretends to be his kin while I sit here wondering about my child. It ain't right, Jack."

"Lotta things ain't right." He slammed the receiver down.

* * *

I enjoyed helping out at Saturday afternoon socials for the Philly neighborhood kids. The children were cut out dolls for a childhood I never had. It kept me from drinking, wondering where the next thrill would be.

"Get out there, darling. Give them all you got," I said.

A skinny-legged girl in pink wasn't afraid of the stage. Her voice was clear but out of tune.

"How'd I do Miss Bessie?"

"You got the muscle, honey, but stop singing to your feet. You on stage to be seen so look at the folks who pay you."

I had so much hope for those children, Philadelphia was hard brick, down in the dumps but a heart like a steel furnace. Those babies were going to rise up somehow and find that ladder to happiness.

I walked home on Worry Street, chatting with neighbors like everything was fine. They thought I had plenty of banked scratch, but truth was the door closed on me like everybody else. Without Richard, it would have been a cold hard time. Long as Tinnie, Viola and the babies were living, no dollar of mine was going to gather dust. Jack had been right about one thing. What did street singing babies like me know about money? I don't cry because I'm the best that the blues has made, but the world put cotton in its ears.

169

Just like the times before this, I headed south and was never refused. Cut the admission so two could go for the price of one. If you entered my tent, I made time stand still. My girls kicked like a machine. If hard work was the measure, everything would have turned out fine. We took the world like we found it hanging around our necks.

"I'm sixty years old, Bessie, missing two fingers from this hand and a thumb from the other. Might live five more years but why should I?" an old friend said.

He didn't expect an answer because he was really talking to the songs. It was my job to worry in public, find words the audience could use when hope was not around. I played those towns that fronted an old dog of a Main Street where roofs gave the only shade, the trees flattened long ago for crops, the air hopeless with heat. Posters curled off buildings where we witnessed to the hung-down heart. The tent, a huge drum lashed tight, housed a third-rate circus with a freak alley, gambling, a Sambo in the Dunk Seat whose simple head would be underwater even if the ball missed the bull's-eye. Couldn't help but grieve the days on my Pullman, my name big as a store sign, free from choosing which lumpy bed was worst. The tents stayed half-full and no town was better than the others. Richard hoped we'd break even. Telegrams from Viola demanded more money NOW, but think she had a word about Snooks? The one thing she could do for me only brought excuses.

My change apron barely held five hundred. Show people can smell a crackup so I bald-faced lied like a sheriff. If need be, we would ditch the cast like I've been ditched. Paid myself first, tiptoed out while the rest slept. They'd been had before. Why didn't they wise up and catch me? I always gave something to the sharp ones.

There is no settling down for me. Nothing to do but to stare at winter skies wishing to be in Shreveport where oil fields glowed. Stars bloated and soft in the smoky mist. The heavy weight of things lives in my shoulder and gin doesn't make it go. A coat hanger replaced my neck. I can't turn and make a getaway. If I had learned to drive, the night would be mine alone. The cold streets would lift me across town. I'd call Playboy but he thinks it's bad luck to be out after four. Time doesn't matter when

170

your number falls. I believe in predestination, that God has it planned whether we believe it or not.

Only freedom we have is to live hard, find the secret of the minutes and seasons while we still got them. There's a seed, a flower growing in the middle of time.

Bessie and Richard Morgan

❧ Chapter 25 ❧

I offered Richard a cigarette. He drove the old Packard smooth and fast through Mississippi. If he was Jack, I would've had to buy at least a '36 Buick to keep up with 1937, but this was the car I loved. The seats were wide enough for me to sleep in. The light brown cloth didn't heat up on the worst days. Richard pulled off the road to pee. I stepped out under summer sky. Wild world of cricket song, rough weeds and sweet hot air. I picked off mosquitoes like a fly catcher. Those long sad fields. I hummed *Got the world in a jug, stopper in my hand.* Richard circled his arm about me and tried to make up. I relaxed and sang full out to the cropper's shacks where postage stamp squares of light glared. They knew it was me.

"Could you live here part of the year?" he asked. I shook my head, "No."

"Mississippi's perfect for Indian Summer. The bugs are dead, always a cool breeze."

"My first husband's buried here," I said. "It's a hardship."

"Why you never said anything before?"

"Some memories slap your face," I said.

"I'm sorry, Bessie. What was his name?"

"Earl Love," I said. "We were through before he got poisoned. His folks moved my stuff to one side of the house and I stayed out of their rooms. They said I had too many men before him but they didn't know our business. Earl knew what to say to keep me but he couldn't go against them. I warned him about his cousins, even went one time to see what they called fun. Grown men shot guns at tree trunks and threw snakes on each other's back. The other wives cried and pleaded but I told the men they better not play with me."

"He died how?" Richard asked.

"We'd busted up years before so I don't know, but it wasn't from a tainted fish like I heard. Who's going to eat a stinking perch? He probably choked on some salty meat while the others were grinding in the bushes."

Earl's body flashed before me in that half-second a memory walks and talks. I didn't tell Richard. He laughs at ghosts. Richard looked away from the road. Earl is past and gone. If I'd been there, he'd still be living.

"Bible got it wrong. Trouble was the first thing God created," Richard said.

I nodded with him. The road glistened ahead. Dirt paths, train tracks, the full heat of July. Richard pointed to the raised table top of grass that held the river back. Richard pulled off the highway so we could neck.

"It's a shame this road doesn't let us see the Mississippi glisten pure and clean."

He knew the river travelled low and dirty but a stranger would never guess it was so close. I wished a moon to fill the sky. I thought about Mama again. When Bud was lowered down, she sang the loudest like he was rising instead of falling. All those years gone. The land and everything on it was flat as a picture while we sped by.

I visited Bud's grave plenty of times. I made a shrine from rocks so I wouldn't forget where he was. When the rains washed the stones away, I stuck a pipe deep as I could drive it. Our cabin died with him because he was the pure love. Who else would you beg to breathe in your ear? I didn't have that baby sweetness, was half grown when I was born. He was the beautiful cup that busted on the floor. Mama said the devil had slipped in when she wasn't looking. If she said "pray," better start.

"If you can't make me feel something, God won't neither," she said.

Don't ask about about dinner on nights like that.

"Never confuse your wishes with God's will," she warned.

My favorite prayer was "Why couldn't she have had more days?"

I said it out loud. Richard heard it. He kissed my nose before starting the car. We slid down Highway 61.

"You're the memory, Bessie."

"Memory of what? I remember too much already."

"Your singing reminds me of my mother walking along the road with a flickering light," Richard said. "She didn't see the stars for worrying about stepping on a snake."

"I'm glad to make people remember their family, but which is better: seeing or feeling a memory?"

"Feeling trumps seeing. Nobody remembers what a kiss looks like except in a movie."

He loved to argue ideas that have no end.

"We feel but still get fooled."

I turned as I spoke. My mouth was dry. An image of eyes bathed in blood frightened me.

"Everything good's a hope"

"You used to say words is words. Now you're talking about hope," I said.

"Have it your way, baby."

"I trust you, Richard. That's more to me than love."

"But you can't see either one, can you?" he said.

"You think I tell everybody I love them?"

"Did you just say you loved me? Thought you trusted me. Is there a difference to you?"

"What's the difference?" I asked.

"I asked first." was his answer.

He felt around for matches, stole glances like a college boy.

"Love's a prayer. It signifies what we can't understand."

I said he was too smart for his own good and put my hand in his lap.

"Giving you something to understand," I said, knowing he was disappointed that I didn't just say I loved him. I weighed my fame with my knee against the dash. I knew a million ears held my verses. It had to be that way.

I asked for a drink, then asked who gave him the flask. He said her name, and we let it ride. Narrow cement highway all to ourselves. A night so dark only portions of his hands and face could be seen. He chain-smoked. I gave the liquor back. The stars were everywhere. A deep summer night, every breeze a masterpiece. The wheels spoke across our thoughts. I curled by the door. The trees cave black against the darkness. Cotton gins were towers in the bare yards.

I refused to be forgotten. Jazz gigs in New York lined up after this trip. Let the crowd discover me again. What I've got don't have a name.

"Everything's coming your way. Bessie. I didn't leave the card game because you made me, I left because I wanted peace. That's what you have had since we hooked up. Tell the truth."

He moved my head toward him with the free hand. I knew he was still kind of mad that I made him leave a stack of chips and his big friends. They sized me up while they paid him and knew he loved me. The car coasted through the slight turns. Tufts of cotton floated free, smeared the wild grasses and few trees. Kudzu glistened silver over phone poles and pines. Cotton stacked in bins, wagons full of cargo tarped and ready for the day.

Richard stopped again but I stayed inside. He gave me a Coca Cola from the cooler on intuition. I felt short-winded and empty. Richard said I sounded like my regular self, but I knew how I felt. The night had barely cooled from the day, mosquitoes bit like snakes.

"Better get me there quick," I said.

"Does Queen Bee want a new driver?"

I gave him a fuck you look but didn't argue. I had to split Memphis. Too many moaning beggars. A girl I used to know was dropping hints. I wasn't fooling with her. When I ignored her, she kept leaning over Richard while serving him drinks. I know what he saw. Cornered her in the toilet and should have kicked her ass down the stairs when she said "all is fair."

He put the car in gear and took the long bridge into deep country. Time is everything for a singer. Words must fall just right. I rubbed the tight creases in his gabardine slacks. His hat was tilted south. A handkerchief in his coat pocket. Shoes a dark red-brown. My man still sharp, dead of night. He knew the towns that didn't print a sign. His speech was jive. Richard would keep up with business while my show was on. I wasn't using up my travel time in barbershops and funeral parlors. Too bad Ma Rainey closed it down; this summer reminded me of the first one with her.

Richard squealed the brakes because the road disappeared into fog, a wet cage that captured us from behind. He drove inside the glowing dewdrops. A clear view opened then closed. I wanted to sleep with Richard while the car was moving. Sit on top of him, let his dick tell my hands how to drive. Steamy white skies, trees flying in and out of existence. I asked him to slow down my damn car.

"You the one who has to get to a closed up town before dawn. What is it you really want?" he said.

My mind followed the clock in Memphis. Twelve minutes past, fifteen, thirty. The second hand got inside me. I had Ma Rainey's letter saying when God comes into a heart, the world changes. Georgia Tom said blues is the grasping for love that can't be. Where's the sweetness in that? he'd asked Ma. She paid no attention until her people started falling sick. Ma provided bags of corn, potatoes, anything called sweet. Her drinking water had to be sugared. I saw her sing *Sweet Is Jesus Name* wearing a tuxedo in a buffet flat, drunk as a lord.

I'd leave the blues but the public wouldn't let me cash out. A sunny day is married to a storm. I thought about the mystery of breath, everything from solid stones to birds. Sometimes I'm a prowling cat, one paw cocked, ready to reconsider my plan. Curious, ready to place a hand where it shouldn't be, renting a room because some eyes must be kissed. The devil's buck naked and his hands are hot. He brought me low so there would be no easy way out. I hurt Jack Gee because he couldn't see me plain. Did the crowd yell for his ass on the stage? Did his period happen in the middle of a kick? My C-notes still in his drawers. I told him love was really wanting, that there was nothing beyond a need. I'd lied about loving him, all I wanted was the old thrill, the lie that a good fuck will give. I didn't love my gowns or my recordings or the money or anything that could be seen. If I loved anything, it was the sound I remembered on a lost day in Chattanooga when Black Patti showed me something new.

I know I'm rough but Jack hit me too hard. Then he complained I couldn't have no babies. I told him I rode his dick long enough to get something beside the clap. Wasn't my fault if he could only piss. He busted a hotel door down and found me sleeping by myself. We still had it because there was a nightie under my pillow too small for me to wear. Who was he to change me five hundred miles from home? I've had everything and now nothing owns me, not even happiness.

"Sing to me," Richard said.

"What do I get for it?"

"A road without an end," he said. I wondered where that highway might be but I sang loud as he could stand it. Just pure sound, shameless emotion. My heart and legs beat steady but memories spoke with the sound. Richard and I disappeared in the silence afterward. We were slow as seasons.

"You're in a carnival again, twenty years later. The Empress of the Blues, top of the bill," he chuckled "Do these motherfuckers know how lucky they are?"

"And this is my kingdom," I waved to the smoky haze.

"You'll never go out of style, Bessie. From the side porch to the shotgun shack, somebody will give you their seat."

"Philadelphia's my home, Richard."

"That's where you live." Richard scrubbed the window with his sleeve. The night turned cool like rain from the sea. The moisture hung for long seconds before falling. We slowed way down.

"What if we could carry the fog in a suitcase," I said. Richard kept driving, like he hadn't heard.

"You think it's possible to hide in that suitcase, Bessie? I don't remember you hiding from anything before."

"I only want a piece of the night for us. I want to be in it like we are now. I want to open the suitcase and the rain and wind and sound from the car will be there when I open it."

"I don't get it. Won't be nothing to see when we arrive. Damn! We've missed the turn-off for the best hole-in-the-wall."

"I don't want to be bothered with other people," I said, imagining a joint full of rounders hoping I'd remember them. Richard wanted to talk, but I rolled the window down to listen to the dull noise.

"Say it plain, baby."

"The word is Clara Smith's was offered the same gig we're headed to. If she thinks my ass is too big to shake, I'll break her heart just like before."

"You want it this bad?" he said.

"What's it sound like? She didn't know what a dream was until she saw my success. She ran up saying 'Help me, Bessie, I'll never forget you', and now she wants to take my place."

"It's nothing but a half-ass sideshow you wouldn't have hired for an opening act."

"It'll look first-class when I take over."

Richard cares, but he don't know my mind. I stay moody. When I sing indoors, the notes are too big for the house. If I sing outdoors, the

179

tramps and preacher come by. I wake up singing but the phone stays dead. He's right, we don't need to be driving all night. The carnivals are never on time. The fog broke clean and smooth. Wind in trees and vines, the noise of the motor. I rolled the window completely down. I touched Richard's arm while he sped into the minutes. I woke up dreaming about Jack Jr., Richard said that I'd never find him until Jack Sr. relented.

"He's mine. He loves me and he's mine. His mother couldn't do for him. I had it all."

"Everything but a baby," Richard said.

The night caught my tears. I told Richard about shopping for Jack Jr. I knew the clerk was scared we might not be able to buy the clothes she laid out. Whites would refuse to buy them if they knew a black kid had wore them.

The clerk boxed everything soon as Snooks tried it on even though I didn't say I was taking it. The counter was full of clothes when I decided on another style. The poor woman went pale. When I finally made the sale she put her hand out real fast.

"That will be cash," loud enough for the whole floor to hear.

"Didn't think you had the money, did they?"

"They weren't sure it was me. You know how we all look alike. That's when being the Empress meant something. The times money made me white."

"I'm glad it's early," he said.

"I'm glad it's just you and me."

"Can't hitch us all behind a plow," Richard said.

I wanted the blue dawn to come light the sky like negatives in Van Vechten's studio. Those chemicals stunk like bad blood. The shadows gathered into mirrors. The dark becoming light like the fog. Out of nothing the morning will be.

"Daylight coming, Bessie."

"This will be a big day," I said.

"Don't get soft, baby. It'll be quite a bit like yesterday."

Richard couldn't let me dream without an argument. I fluttered my hand like the church people and he allowed my silence. We turned where the road sloped west. The grade was easy, the only all-night station before the Delta was like a buoy on the ocean.

"The white boy pumping the gas knows you," Richard said. I turned to see a git-box lay on the steps of the filling station.

"He wants you to listen at him."

I said ok but wasn't leaving the car. The boy dipped his head. He played a good blues a little too fast. He riffed on a major to a diminished. I hummed with him without planning and he floated up and down in his shoes. The hard light over the pumps spotted us like targets. The country sounds, a cow, the nervous horses and lost bird calls.

"Damn if this don't beat everything," the boy said over and over. We left him resting his hands on the guitar neck, its redness raw against the pumps.

"He's still standing there, Bessie," Richard said as we drove away. I was hungry. The boy awakened my voice so I sang.

My fingers played time. I shook in the seat like steps were possible. The hot glow of horns brightened the road. I heard applause, saw the wild hands beating air.

"Richard, why you drive so slow?" I said.

The night was a wild place. I awoke and felt like I was flying away. The windows were empty. The car threaded a hole in the fog no wider than a sleeve. Richard said I'd been meek for an hour and now I was hell again. Him, who'd I'd been practically an angel with. I'd been too nice. Believed in him and all that shit because he could stay up all night and go to breakfast. Believed because he didn't have a fit if a girl invited me for a drink. Didn't even ask to watch. He didn't want nobody else so I didn't drag scandals home, but now he seemed like the rest of them.

"What's the matter, baby?" he said.

I wasn't falling for it. The car was mine. The slow pace was his. The fog was sent to hem me in. If I had a shotgun, I'd clear the highway of all ideas but my own. There was a pounding on the other side of the car door. I wondered why Richard didn't answer it.

"Do you love me, Richard?," I said.

"Why do you think I'm here?" he said.

"That's not good enough," I said. I wanted more. I wanted an explanation of my birth. I asked him for the weight of wild seeds.

"Do you believe in me, Bessie?"

The car hit uneven places in the road. The roaring in my ears was worse. I yelled to make him hear me. We argued at each other. Our breath pearled the windshield. I rolled the window down. The wet night slowed my thoughts. Could I roll out of the car and live? Richard pulled over. He held me but said nothing. The silence was draped in a clouded tent big as the morning. I dreamed we walked for hours but couldn't find my show. He nuzzled my ears with memories of our first days together. He smelled of tobacco and good cologne.

"I must love you baby, because I ain't mad about anything," I said.

Richard pulled back on the road. He drove left-handed so one hand would always touch me. He told me the world was still mine.

I was asleep when the wheels locked. I knew we were flying out of the skid. The door exploded. My bones were dry ice. Richard cursed and cried out. The car flew backward, then straight up. My neck snapped back and I couldn't speak. An explosion. Falling. Metal. I waited for the the loudest sound to end. My whole body was wet. A red comet for an arm. Smoke and metal. My eyes would not open and my voice was flat as paper. I was so far from words. I had broken apart. No knees would obey me. The heavy wheel rattled and spun. It cried like a cheap clarinet. Richard repeated my name. I wanted to say cold cement had no mystery at all. I wanted to argue about the accommodations. My blood was everywhere. I had never felt such hurt. I can't say "tomorrow." Richard is a good man but he gets distracted. I wanted to soak him in peacefulness. I heard somebody play my records one after the other. My dead Mama said each one was better than the last and she never heard any of them. I told her the companies didn't want me but I would sing all night whenever she wanted. Why doesn't somebody help Richard? He's hysterical with my name.

"I'm here, Richard. It's Bessie, the one you love."

It's simple now but you don't understand. Please don't move me. If I play dead, the pain floats in a lake between my ribs. Don't shake me, Richard. If I overflow, I'm gone. The fog rolls down and pulls back smoke. Gasoline in my hair. Why doesn't Daddy come for me?

Richard spoke. The road, the trees, and sky fell on my shoulder. The world leaned against an empty wall. If I wanted, I could slide for years.

I knew this was coming. All my life I knew. I dared death to come rather than be scared. Remembered when that rounder put his dick in me, I wasn't but twelve years old. That slobber he put on it didn't help me none. Hate saved me then. What will save me now?

Thought it would be a bullet. It almost was a knife. I didn't want nobody but a true few. I learned my reasons to save myself. All my people dead. Come on then, welcome me. I'm waiting for the love that don't never change.

I wasn't afraid of nothing. I had my dives, my parties where the cops refuse to go. Find me where the Negroes hang off the edge of rivers, walk between moving trains. Who cares if we fall? Dragged myself out of third billing greasy as a card game. Wore the heartbroken clothes you paid to see. I remember every song but time has stopped.

Richard remembered the beady-eyed taillights. He tried to fly the Packard but hit the back end of the other car. The people who sped away saw us skid and flip. They heard. Why didn't they at least stop? Richard came to on a broken door.

"Please help me, Mister. That's Bessie Smith," Richard said. The man's car had parked on the highway several yards from Bessie's car, headlights still on.

"The singer?" The second white man looked around.

"The other car was moving too slow. I thought it was going my speed," Richard said hoping for help.

"I'm a doctor," the stranger said. He clicked on his flashlight. "Jesus, God, her arm is about off."

My man said "Richard Morgan," to the doctor. Said he was in business for himself. He was Bessie's traveling companion. He leaned over the doctor and was pushed away.

Richard hoped she was dead. The doctor listened on his knees and Richard heard Bessie breathe. The beats echoed. He knew her sounds were shallow. Richard turned round and round, his hands touching and rubbing himself.

I told Richard fame can't bring anybody back to life. He said nobody expected it to. I couldn't make his mind rest. I told him to talk louder. I heard fluttering wings. Then one dirty wing inside the car, another one outside the window. The wild feathers rose and fell. Boxes of leaves filled the car. There wasn't any room for seats, windows. They covered me.

Not a minute of forgiveness was expected. I used to be excited by trouble, would have stacked chairs on top of the leaves to see everything but we all run short of time no matter how good our preparation. We always want that little bit longer at the shore, that minute that will never be.

The doctor told Richard it would be more help if he stood off the road. Richard drove us to the middle of hell but it wasn't on purpose. The doctor asked Richard if he was drunk. The second white man acted like he knew our story. Richard had two quick ones hours ago. The doctor knew he was sober. This is Mississippi, so Richard held up and wouldn't cry. The doctor's friend ran to find a house with a phone.

Richard whispered "please get up." He said it until his tongue froze.

The doctor kept checking my pulse. Richard knew that I couldn't speak any more but the white man had all the education. The fog whipped in and out. Richard wanted to help when the friend came back, but they still motioned against him. When I cried out, Richard hollered, "Don't hurt her no more." He put his hands over his ears to silence the sounds from my wounds.

Richard yelled "Ambulance!" He heard my voice like it was an hour before. He told of miracles. The friend stood on the running board of the doctor's car trying to see. I lay in the road beside the old Packard. The ambulance climbed the dips and leveled, the fog snowy white with pieces of trees sticking through. The headlights grew brighter, but no siren.

"Dammit, they ain't stopping, Doc. Get off the road. This ain't no ambulance."

"You can't help her being dead," the doctor said and ran past Richard.

Richard ran too. The men yelled "Stop!" The speeding car hit the doctor's Ford that was slanted across the road then spun into the Packard. None of the cars touched me. I was like before. The doctor's rolls of bandages spooled out like ribbons. People in the new car moaned from their injuries. A young white fellow fell cursing and puking. Richard rubbed my face to show he was still there. I was clammy and hot at the same time. He lay down on the highway with me. The others let us be. It was our last bed. He said my face was perfect, not a scrape or damage. He said the hospital wasn't far. He knew I was gone but couldn't let go.

The doctor motioned for help, but Richard's muscles had become straw. They somehow lifted me off the road. My strand of pearls rolled free and Richard didn't try to find them. The doctor and the white couple that just crashed talked among themselves. When the first ambulance came, the doctor opened the door for the white couple then watched it speed off.

The colored ambulance rolled up after while. Blood red lights blazed while Richard and them struggled to get me onto the gurney. Vast rays from the early sun flattened the land.

When they got Bessie to Clarksdale, the black doctor had to cut off her arm. He doubled the morphine but wasn't no use. Richard couldn't speak clearly. He didn't care what anybody thought of Richard Morgan.

"We drove all night for this? She made me bring her, I didn't want to come, I was winning big. My hand was flush. I have no talent except to recognize talent. Why ain't I dead?" he said to windows, floor and self.

The room she died in provided plenty of company. Richard wasn't the only one sitting up with family. They let them smoke in there. The hallway ended at a screen door that overlooked where wild reeds and saplings drank from a slow stream. He leaned on the railing and cried. Last year, he and Bessie went into the bright red juke across the street from the hospital. Richard had walked in front of her. They heard the joint before seeing it across the field. Its slatted windows were wide open. Small groups of people stood outside of the building. The music was a single voice and guitar.

"Miss Bessie's here," the shout went up. She shook hands, told them she'd never stop singing long as they wanted to hear.

He came back to real time. Just him and Bessie. Richard bought half a bottle from somebody. He thought about giving her a taste but dipped his fingers in the water-glass instead to moisten her silent lips. Just them two in that narrow room with the lowest ceiling in the world. She wouldn't hate him for drinking while she died. He shook in spasms when the nurses wheeled her away. You don't know what he lost.

He denied being drunk to the sheriff's face. He expected they'd jail him to take his money, but they let him go. The crying porters let him sit in the baggage car with the body far as Chicago before the conductor made him take a regular seat on the Philadelphia-bound line. She would have wanted him there for the funeral and so he went. Ten thousand people and the one she loved stayed at the back of the funeral home. Jack Gee tried to fall on her casket sobbing about the love like heaven, but Maud blocked him out. People feared Richard might snap.

"I should have married her, but she feared a jinx on us. Our days were alive and no one could tear us down," Richard recalled.

"Why risk it? Put your name on mine and the driving wheel might break. Never would have happened if we'd left it alone," Bessie had said.

He went to his home with her belongings. He laid them on tables, on the bed. He listened to her sing and couldn't be satisfied.

If her music is a prayer, that's because God let blues tell the story. Some say all what black folk been through was finally heard when she was on stage. If that's the reason for her fame, the shortness of her time, the sad end can't just be about her. Those songs were another chance, an end to sadness that isn't death.

There's a room on the side of the road. Waiting for her. She crawls downstairs, crosses the muddy stream. Her name was Bessie and she remembers everything.

Grave Unmarked

At the beginning of the Bessie Smith revival in 1970, her grave was found in Philadelphia—unmarked . . . unmarked although Bessie in later life had been rolling in money.

A nurse who used to scrub Bessie Smith's kitchen when the nurse was a little girl offered to pay half the cost—whatever it happened to be—and rock singer Janis Joplin paid the other half, bill unseen. The monument company refused any profit.

Miss Joplin did not attend the unveiling, those close to the situation feeling that the rock star wanted to emphasize that her involvement was not for publicity, but out of respect.

CPSIA information can be obtained
at www.ICGtesting.com
Printed in the USA
BVHW090501211221
624509BV00011B/604